MORE NEW GAMES!

A Headlands Press Book

MORE NEW GAMES!

...and Playful Ideas from the New Games Foundation

Text and photographs by Andrew Fluegelman

Dolphin Books / Doubleday & Company, Inc.
Garden City, New York / 1981

Created with the assistance and support of the New Games Foundation, San Francisco, California

Consulting editor: Nancy Kretz
Editorial board: Pam Cleland, Bill Michaelis,
  Ray Murray
Contributors: Bill Barr, Betsy Brown, Adrienne Burk,
  Steve Butler, Pam Cleland, Kate Douglas, Fred
  Evers, Bill Healey, Nancy Kretz, John LaRue, Ken
  Leary, Larry Loebig, Jeff McKay, Bill Michaelis,
  Burton Naiditch, Kathryn Parker, John Rippey, Bill
  Rubin, Gail Straub, Todd Strong, Marcelle Weed,
  John Wertz, Karen Wolf, Tom Zink
Additional photography: Betsy Brown, p. 183; Nancy
  Kretz, p. 186; Ray Murray, p. 182

Produced by The Headlands Press, Inc.,
Tiburon, California

Project editor: Andrew Fluegelman
Designer: Howard Jacobsen
Text editor: Susan Brenneman
Photographic prints: Emilio Mercado
Composition: Sara Schrom, Type by Design,
  Fairfax, California
Mechanical production: Craig DuMonte
Printing and binding: George Banta Company,
  Menasha, Wisconsin

Library of Congress Cataloging in Publication Data
Fluegelman, Andrew, 1943–
More new games! . . . and playful ideas from the New
Games Foundation.
"A Headlands Press book."
Includes index.
1. Games. 2. Amusements. I. New Games
Foundation. II. Title.
GV1201.F57   794   81-9692
ISBN 0-385-17514-0   AACR2

10 9 8 7 6 5 4

N 0-385-17514-0>>995

To everyone who's ever said,
"Let's play a new game!"

Contents

More Than a List of Games

When we at the *New Games Foundation introduced our first collection of games in* The New Games Book, *in 1976, we extended an invitation: "Play them, change them, have fun with them." But none of us imagined then just how many people would take us up on that invitation.* More New Games! *is the result of five years' worth of playing, experimenting, and having fun. It's a sampling of the best new* New Games *and playful ideas we've collected from more than a million players, reflecting boundless energy and countless smiles.*

More New Games! *is also a product of the hundreds of trainings, workshops, and festivals we've conducted in cities across North America and in Europe and Australia. As we've responded to the needs of human-services professionals and group leaders (and people simply interested in experiencing play for its own sake), we've refined our own approach to play. In* More New Games! *we hope to share some of the practical suggestions and useful techniques—as well as the creative and joyful moments—that have arisen out of these many and diverse New Games events.*

At every New Games gathering we play, of course, so we're presenting sixty new New Games for you to try. As with our first book, we've grouped the games according to the most appropriate number of participants and approximate activity level. This organization should help get you started choosing games to suit the players you have on hand. But we hope you'll soon discover that most of the games can be adapted for more or fewer players, or made more or less active, simply by altering the rules a bit. New Games are meant to be your games. If a game isn't right for you, change it! Throughout this book, we offer suggestions for personalizing the games, making them fit your needs and tastes.

Are these New Games different in nature from those in our first book? Not significantly. They all involve some physical activity and seek to get as many people as possible playing. Users of The New Games Book might discover, however, that these games embody more fully the New Games style of play: They are more easily adaptable to a wide range of players; they are richer in elements of fantasy and ritual; they build a stronger play community. Most importantly, we think you'll find these games as much fun as those in our first collection.

New Games represent more than a list of games, however. They provide an approach to recreation and play that transcends the boundaries of any game. In the four essays in this book, we've attempted to help you apply New Games and make them come to life in your park, gym, or backyard. "An Attitude Toward Play" is a guide to the New Games philosophy. You'll discover that any game can be a New Game if you make the interests of the players more important than the game itself.

"Tag, You're It!" offers some practical suggestions for leading and playing New Games, as well as for adapting and inventing games. "The Big Game" is a collection of New Games true adventures that illustrate the many settings in which New Games have been applied successfully, from traditional sports programs to community recreation, special-population services, churches, camps, businesses, and community organizations. For those of you interested in pursuing New Games further, we've provided some information about the New Games Foundation and its programs in "After the Fourth Tournament."

The one aspect of New Games we can't adequately present in any book is the sheer magic that comes from playing together in an atmosphere of trust and freedom. To experience that magic, you can't just read about New Games— you have to play them. You don't need any special equipment, or an elaborate playing field or gym. You don't have to be in shape. You don't have to worry about being a superstar. All you have to do is gather a few of your friends and let playfulness become part of your lives.

So to old New Gamesters, newcomers, and passers-by, we're extending our invitation once again. Please join us playing more New Games! ■

Games for Two

HIGH ACTIVITY

Toe Fencing
Crab Grab
Human Spring

MEDIUM ACTIVITY

Me Switch
Quick Draw
Butt Off

LOW ACTIVITY

Commons
This Is My Nose
Last Detail

Toe Fencing

This game may have been invented in the 1950s when two rivals attempted to scuff each other's freshly powdered white bucks. It has recently enjoyed a renaissance among white-shoed tourists waiting for the cable cars in San Francisco.

To play, we face each other, holding hands. Then we try to tap the tops of each other's toes with our own. When one of us scores three hits, it's time to switch to a new partner.

The frenzy generated by Toe Fencing places a premium on honest self-refereeing—the name of the game is *not* Toe Stomping. Players should be equally armed—barefeet to barefeet, sneakers to sneakers, moccasins to moccasins—and we do not advise playing in steel-toed boots or six-inch spike heels unless everyone is equipped with shin guards.

Who knows? Toe Fencing just might be the next *American Bandstand* craze. ∎

Crab Grab

This is a crustacean-inspired contest of the grab-and-grapple variety that definitely allows us to fulfill the "play hard" part of the New Games credo.

We assume the classic crab position—bellies up, elbows and knees bent, bodies elevated on hands and feet. We must maintain this position—supported by at least three extremities—while each of us tries to make the other touch his rear end to the ground.

The rest of the rules are for us to create. We can allow players to make contact only with their feet, or we can allow hand-to-hand or foot-to-hand or perhaps body-to-body contact too. It all depends on whether we want the game to be very active, extremely active, or totally exhausting.

The crab position offers a mode of locomotion that can be incorporated into many other games. All it requires is a strong constitution and a soft surface. We should keep in mind, however, that some people are allergic to shellfish. ■

Human Spring

This game is a corollary to the game of Stand-Off, which appeared in *The New Games Book*. Instead of trying to upset each other's balance, what happens if we try our best to keep each other upright?

We stand with our feet spread at shoulders' width, facing each other about an arm's distance apart. We hold our hands up in front of us, palms facing forward. Now, keeping our bodies as rigid as possible, we lean forward at the same time, catching each other with our palms and rebounding to a standing position with a springlike action.

If that was too easy, we can both take a short step back and try again. We've now got a longer distance to fall and spring back, so more challenge and more trust are involved. We can keep stepping back until we reach the point where our human spring is in danger of becoming a human sprung.

Human Spring should be played on a soft surface, or for a change of environment, how about trying it in water? ∎

Me Switch

You never know—that person sitting next to you on the airplane, the bus, or the train just might be the source of a great game. This one-on-one contest was passed on to us by a traveling friend who learned it from a ten-year-old he met about 10,000 feet above the Rockies in a plane headed west. They played nonstop till the Sierra.

First, we must master the game's three signals: (1) hands angled above the eyebrows; (2) one hand pointed up and the other sideways, touching the opposite elbow; (3) both hands crossed in front of the chest.

One of us starts by saying, "Me, switch!" At the word *switch*, we snap into one of the three signals. The object is for the caller to trap his opponent into making the *same* signal he did.

If there's no match, we switch roles, and whoever was the noncaller immediately starts the next round with, "Me, switch!" We each snap into one of the signals again, and the call keeps alternating until there is a match. Three matches by one of us wins (if we're playing for baseball cards).

This game is best played ultrafast, with each "Me, switch!" "Me, switch!" "Me, switch!" coming right after the other. It quickly becomes such an eyeball-to-eyeball psych-out showdown that we may find ourselves playing coast to coast. ∎

Quick Draw

Here's a way to turn any spare moment into an instant B western.

We face each other, hands at our sides, until one of us starts the game by jerking his hands into either a finger-pointing or a hands-up position. The other of us has to respond immediately — simultaneously, really — with the countermove. Whoever starts the action tries to trap his partner into making the *same* move he did. When that happens, we switch roles and the stick-'em-up action continues.

The best thing about Quick Draw is that it knows no time limits. Once we've initiated play, either of us is fair game for a sudden round, anytime, anywhere. We'll have to stay on guard at the bus stop, the supermarket, and the dinner table, and we can keep score forever. ■

Butt Off

Here's a posterior variation of Stand-Off (from *The New Games Book*) in which having the best playing equipment is not nearly as important as skillfully using what we do have.

We stand back to back (more accurately, butt to butt), with our feet spread about shoulders' width. We start with a ritual count to three, swaying to the right and left while maintaining our cheek-to-cheek position; then we try to knock each other

off balance. The only permissible hit in this game is a moderately gentle bun bunt. Balance and strategy, of course, come into play. Be forewarned (or aft-warned): Whoever hits first may get the upper hind.

We can also try a variation in which we start with our rear ends touching and try to push each other over while maintaining *gluteus maximal* contact.

A note for traveling New Games players: On the East Coast, this game might be encountered as Summa Derrière, except around New York City, where it's usually called Tush Push. ■

Commons

Despite its name, this game has very little in common with any other sane form of human activity. That's why it's a perfect way to let everyone know right from the start that we play New Games just for fun.

First, we decide on three sound-and-motion signals—the sillier the better, of course. We might try a turkey gobble with our fingers flapping next to our ears, or maybe a Bronx cheer performed with our thumbs deftly placed on our noses. Or how about a descending-dive-bomber whistle terminating in a digital explosion?

Once we've agreed on the signals, the rest of the game is a snap (and Snap is an alternative name for this game). We turn back to back, count to three, and spin to face each other while we each make one of the signals. If we make the same signal, we've won, so to speak, and we can move on to our next playful pursuit. But if we find ourselves facing each other with two different forms of silliness, we've got to turn around and try again. (Most pairs manage to match up in the first 397 tries.)

This foolish frolic need not be confined to two. Everyone in a group can pair off and play Commons until there's one persistent partnership still trying to get it together. (Give them a cheer when they do.) We can also play in threes or in three teams. In the latter version, each team comes up with one sound-and-motion signal. When everyone perfects all three signals, the teams huddle and decide which to perform, on cue, *as a team*. A three-team match wins it for everyone.

By the time we manage to unite ourselves with finger popping, ear stopping, and razzmatazz, we'll surely be joined in purely playful common cause. ◼

This Is My Nose

How should we respond when someone approaches us, sticks his finger in his ear, and says, "This is my nose"? Chances are, he's not attempting to transmit an obscure message, but merely extending an invitation to play this New Game.

One of us could quite properly respond to him by tugging her chin and saying, "This is my ear." Then he could continue the game by scratching his head and claiming, "This is my chin." And she might then pat her butt and insist, "This is my head."

Undoubtedly, some onlooker will wisecrack that these two are in bad shape if they can't tell one end from the other. We should explain to him that the object of this ultimate test of hand-eye-mouth coordination is to say the body part the other person has just pointed to, while pointing to another body part. Then we should challenge him to a game and see how long he can keep the chain going before his tongue gets twisted with his anatomy. ∎

Last Detail

With most New Games, we don't have to concern ourselves with the precise rules. We can adapt this detective game to different situations too, but it's definitely one in which we have to be sticklers for detail.

We start by facing each other (one to one or team to team) and remaining still for two or three minutes. But we should not let the time pass idly; instead, we should be doing our best to observe and remember as much as we can about the person facing us.

We then turn our backs to each other and change six details about the way we look—details that can be seen without the need to touch or move anything. Once rearranged, we turn back to face each other and see whether we can spot all the changes in our partners.

That sneaky fellow in the photos has changed his appearance in six ways. Can you spot every last detail? ■

An Attitude Toward Play

Play hard, play fair, nobody hurt." It's been the New Games motto since the first New Games Tournament, in 1973, and it still stands for our essential purpose—to celebrate play by making the players the most important part of the game.

As we've shared more games with diverse players, our philosophy has taken shape. We've come to better understand the relation between competition and cooperation. We've seen that games can involve psychological risks as well as physical risks. We've experienced the power of play to remove us from the everyday world and unite us in a unique community.

In the pages that follow, we'll draw upon our list of games to identify the major elements of the New Games philosophy. In one sense, we'll be highlighting the various components that make a game a New Game. But we'll also move beyond an analysis of specific games toward an understanding that what New Games are really about is an attitude toward play—a way of playing—and that attitude can work for the old games we've played for years as well as the new games we've yet to invent.

Challenge. *In New Games we emphasize challenge rather than competition. Sometimes this causes a misunderstanding: "New Games? Oh, you mean noncompetitive games." There are, of course, many New Games that are noncompetitive—Cookie Machine and Yurt Circle, for example. But anyone who has raced around the outside of the wheel in the game Broken Spoke knows that he was in hot competition for a spot back in the spoke formation. And all of us on the bus during Pushpin Soccer were furiously competing with our opponents for balloons to bat into*

the popping range of our respective goalies. A New Game may or may not be competitive—but all New Games are definitely challenging.

Sometimes a New Game challenges an entire group to achieve one goal, as in our collective attempt to end up in the same chair in Pile Up. Other New Games challenge us as individuals. In Swat, for example, we compete on a one-to-one basis. Group Juggling challenges each individual to

accomplish a goal shared by the group. Star Wars, on the other hand, presents a more traditional challenge—that of competing teams that rely on individual skills and cooperative group effort.

In New Games, however, we don't just believe in emphasizing challenge. We also believe that the challenges of any game should be meaningful to all the players, so that the players remain the focus of the game.

We provide broad-based challenges in New Games in a number of different ways. We try to design games that demand a variety of skills from the players. Many New Games require traditional sports skills such as speed, strength, coordination, and quick reflexes. But these games might also be won with brainpower, through strategy. And there are many games that demand a sense of humor, acting talent, or other forms of what we call creative play. In a game like Octopus, a player can elude the slimy hold of the octopus's tentacles with quick reactions and quick feet, but he can also swim safely through the ocean by hanging back, picking a route, using his powers of observation to avoid being tagged. In Tableaux, creative acting wins the day. And in a game like Lemonade, good runners, good actors, good guessers, and good strategists can all shine.

In the games that do depend largely on physical skills, New Games tempers the competitive spirit with a spirit of cooperation. Many kinds of New Games provide us with the opportunity to express aggressive or even hostile behavior in a safe context—what one of the originators of New Games, Stewart Brand, termed

softwar. It's fun to engage in the kind of combat required by games like Taffy Pull and Wink. But we don't let ourselves get so caught up in the goal of winning the game that we miss the joy of the challenge. In a softwar game, we don't merely try to overpower our opponents. Instead, we use what we call caring restraint—that is, only as much force or effort as is necessary to meet our opponents' efforts. This preserves the physical challenge of the game for weaker players and creates a different challenge—that of finding the competitive balance—for stronger players.

In all New Games, we broaden the scope of the challenges by tailoring the games to each specific group of players. In How Do You Do?, the players can run around the circle on their way home, but it may work better to send them around at a walk or a hop. There are many suggestions for modifying challenges included in this book—in the games descriptions themselves and in the section on adapting games in the essay "Tag, You're It!"

By emphasizing challenge over competition in New Games, we de-emphasize the importance of the outcome of the games. We applaud

effort as much as (or more than) we applaud success. We design games to fulfill our desire for challenge rather than to separate those who can meet a particular challenge from those who can't. We design them to actually shift the focus away from who won and who lost. One of the ingenious aspects of the game of Wink is the way the roles switch after each round. Regardless of the outcome of a particular confrontation, each player involved is still actively in the game. The individual matches continually shift, so there's no way (or need) to identify who did better or worse. Yet there's no doubt that Wink is a challenging, active—yes, even competitive—game.

We wouldn't have "play hard" in our motto if we didn't want people to try to win. We all want the chance to run as fast as we can, to hold on as tightly as we can, or to be as quick, clever, or funny as we can. But in New Games, we never forget that we're playing together so that the challenge will be there for each of us. Achieving that goal is the only winning that counts.

Trust. *New Games is committed to providing play experiences for the benefit and enjoyment of everyone involved. Because of past experiences, however, some of us may think of games as vehicles only for the skilled few who play just to win, just to defeat others. Some of us may avoid playing games because we're afraid that we won't make the team or that we'll lose or look foolish. In New Games, we send everyone a clear message that we want them to play with us and we want them to feel good about playing. We do it by designing and playing games in a way that expresses a caring attitude—that is, we establish trust as the basis of play.*

In some cases, New Games are designed and played primarily to create and communicate trust. Willow in the Wind is an example. In it, the willow is encouraged to close her eyes, to lean past her balancing point, to let herself be supported by the rest of the players. Once we've experienced giving or receiving such caring support in a trust game, we can carry it into games with more competitive challenges.

Knock Your Socks Off is designed to be a competitive and potentially rough softwar game. A caring attitude is expressed in the way we play it, by exercising restraint even though we're battling to stay in the game. Such caring restraint equalizes the game's challenges and therefore opens it to a wider range of players, and that's one of the goals of New Games. It also lessens the game's dangers—another New

Games goal. And a game that is played safely, with restraint where necessary, creates an atmosphere of trust.

Another more subtle example of caring restraint and support, and the trust they engender, can occur in a game like Swat. Let's say one player has been the swatter for several rounds and is getting so tired that it has become almost impossible for him to make a tag. In New Games, it's everyone's responsibility to see the situation and remedy it without humiliating the tired swatter. We can let ourselves be tagged or modify the game to let the swatter switch roles. Even a bit of creative cheating might be in order. However we exercise restraint and support, the tired swatter can trust us to do something to keep him from being the swatter forever.

Establishing a sense of community, a sense of belonging, is another way New Games engenders trust. In Name Train, we each receive a personalized cheer, our own welcome into the play community. Trust games like Willow in the Wind and Yurt Circle also create a sense of belonging and community. We like games that build alliances among players because alliances build trust. Some alliances are physical, in games such as Loose

Caboose or Quick Lineup; others are associational, in games such as Data Processing or Psychic Shake.

We also create trust when we do our best not to put people on the spot. We ask for volunteers to play special roles in a game—to be It, for instance—and we make choosing sides a game so no one is singled out as the last to be chosen. In elimination games such as Octopus, we don't feel compelled to play on to the last survivor while the rest of us just watch. In games where players perform, we can have them do it in twos, as in Behavior Modification, because there is safety in numbers. And when individuals are spotlighted, in Instant Replay or Killer, for example, the impact is lessened because the spotlight hits everyone at least once in the round.

We take special care not to single out or exclude losers. Losing in a game like Elephant/Palm Tree/ Monkey means making a foolish error. But foolishness is what makes that game fun. No score is kept, and losers always get another chance. In Zen Clap, when someone misses a signal, she gets a new role to play as a heckler. In Monarch, players who get hit with the ball join the team that inevitably

will win. In Giants/Elves/Wizards, players shift from team to team, but everyone stays in the game. Even in a game such as Knock Your Socks Off, which by its nature requires that players be eliminated from the field, the de-soxed players become referees, and we can cloak those roles with such ritual and creative participation that the play community continues to function as a unified group.

So this is what we mean when we say "play fair." We're talking about more than just following rules. We mean that we're not going to use any game to embarrass anyone, or make them feel like a loser or wish they hadn't played with us at all. Whatever the game, it's up to each of us to demonstrate our support for every player. Only in an atmosphere of unqualified trust can a truly playful spirit thrive.

Safety. The third part of our motto is "nobody hurt." We can't be expected to accept challenges and turn our fears into trust if we're concerned about our physical well-being. Although we try to structure physically active New Games to minimize obvious physical dangers, the safety of such games depends primarily on how they are refereed and played.

We've come up with a checklist of safety considerations for New Games—five words that all begin with the letter c. A safe game should be contained, cushioned, controlled, and played with a sense of caring and community. Each of these factors is the responsibility of the game leaders and the players.

A risky game is contained with regard to physical space—that is, the area in which risks are undertaken is clearly delineated. A good example is an intense softwar game like Knock Your Socks Off. We define the playing area by spreading a parachute or mat on the ground, or using boundary markers. The players know that while they are in the area, they assume the physical challenges of the game. They also know that they can leave the area and remove themselves from the risks.

Permitting exit from the game is another aspect of containment. Before a game that might involve physical problems or risks for some players, we clearly explain the situation and extend an invitation not to play. Before playing Jamaquack, for example, we let people know that they'll be bending over (not to mention quacking and keeping their eyes shut!). In Jamaquack, players have the option to remain upright as part of the outer circle.

A New Game that involves physical risk is also contained with regard to entrance by players. When players who don't know the rules and the conventions of the game rush into play, they may injure themselves or others. We invite everyone to play, but only after they understand how we play. This caution is particularly important when we play with special items of equipment such as the Earthball or when we play softwar games.

A safe play area is cushioned. Before playing an active game outdoors, we walk the area to check for holes, sprinkler heads, glass, or other hazards. Indoors, we need to be aware of the playing surface, structural supports, projections, and the like. In some cases, it may be enough to make everyone aware of these hazards. But we might have to play on a mat or move the game to a new location or postpone playing that particular game.

Players must take care to eliminate physical hazards in their apparel. In running games or those that involve physical contact, everyone wears soft-soled shoes. In a game such as Cookie Machine, we remove any sharp jewelry, watches, belt buckles, and breakable eyeglasses before playing.

A game is controlled when we agree on, and play by, the rules. In New Games, the referees are the players, all the players, and ideally, they monitor themselves as much or more than they monitor others. In very active games, however, it's often necessary to have someone remain outside the game, too, monitoring it for safety. In a game like Body Snatchers, in which the players have their eyes closed, we have one or two referees outside the game to keep people from wandering into obstacles or out of bounds.

In very active softwar games, we add another measure of control by incorporating what we call the Stop Rule. If, at any point in the game, any one of us feels in physical danger, we call out "Stop!" Any player hearing that word repeats it and ceases playing. With everyone attuned to this command, a rough game can quickly be brought to a halt and the danger removed or the injury dealt with.

The last two safety factors are caring and community. These qualities are part of the trusting attitude we foster in New Games, and this aspect of the way we play avoids injuries more effectively than rules or physical precautions.

Before any active game, we reiterate the principle of caring restraint—we'll use only the force necessary to match that of our opponents. We also establish the play community by playing several trust games before launching into rougher games.

"Nobody hurt" is not a guarantee. There are risks in any physical activity, and unfortunately, injuries do occasionally occur. But we can greatly reduce those risks by taking a few precautions, by making concern for safety an integral part of the way we play, and by making the well-being of our fellow players the focus of the game.

Fantasy and Ritual. *The list of New Games is rich in imagery and make-believe. When we decide to be samurai or snowmen or locomotives in a switchyard, we're taking a giant step out of the everyday world. We're creating a special place for ourselves—a playground—where we can let ourselves go and be truly free, where we can act in any way, without connection to or consequence in the real world. Fantasies can make a game come alive and at the same time remind us that being captured by a giant or pulled under by an alligator is, after all, just a game. Fantasy is the essence of play.*

Rituals also draw us into the play world, and we look for opportunities to incorporate songs, chants, noise, body movements, and unique conventions in our games. Some of this ritual is fantasy's helper. In How Do You Do?, the handshakes and introductions set

up the party fantasy; in Samurai Warrior, the bows and yells are essential to the make-believe; and Cookie Machine would lose most of its flavor without cries of "Chocolate chip!" or "Macaroon!" In other games, the ritual has more practical uses as well. In Quick Lineup, the raising of hands and the victory shout signify a team's achievement, and they are elements that give drama and closure to the game. And in Snowblind, the chant permits the snowman chain to locate the free players and sets a time limit for changing positions, as well as defining the game's fantasy.

The power of fantasy and ritual is strongest when we really stretch our imaginations as well as our bodies in creative play. In order to cross over into the privileged world of make-believe we must do more than simply say we're something we are not. In Loose Caboose, we can't just claim to be locomotives, we must visualize the steam rising, and the track stretching off to the horizon as we shuffle along, chugging and choochooing, being locomotives. This point is immediately clear in creative-play games like Tableaux—the more we get into being groceries in a checkout-stand tableau, the better the game will work and the more fun it will be. And in a game like Clam Free, playing the role of nuclear reactor or irradiated clam can give a game of tag impact, meaning, and life.

Once we've all tried being a locomotive, a grocery bag, or a nuclear reactor, we realize that the freedom that fantasy and ritual confers on us is the freedom to be silly, to act out. How often do we walk backward with our heads between our legs, eyes closed, quacking? Who ever even heard of a jamaquack? And where else but in a game like Samurai Warrior could we unleash our hostilities and our sword-fighting fantasies? We rarely get such opportunities to be utterly foolish or to indulge our alter egos. Fantasy and ritual can provide a joyful release as we cast aside our concerns for self-image.

Fantasy can also provide an alternative to purely physical challenge in games. Games like Mime Rhyme and Lemonade make the acting and guessing of fantasy or imagery the central focus of the game. And role playing is also integral to Willow in the Wind, Taffy Pull, and Body Surfing. By making silliness or fantasy an important element in a game, we're letting each other know in a dramatic way that we're not taking the outcome of the game too seriously.

Successfully tapping into the power of fantasy requires a special emphasis on the atmosphere of trust we strive for in New Games and on our commitment to balanced challenges. A player may find assuming fantastical identities or quacking upside down to be quite difficult and threatening, especially if there are players around who transform themselves into octopuses or balloons at the drop of a hat. We may need to balance the challenge for our more reluctant actor by giving him a partner or by working up to full-scale fantasy performances, like a Killer death scene, by first engaging in group fantasies, like Giants/Elves/Wizards, or group theater games, like Tableaux. Most of all, as players we must genuinely permit each other to be as silly and as free as fantasy will permit. We must be as sensitive and gentle with leaps of fancy as we are with leaps of the body.

Every game creates and is created by its rituals and fantasies. In New Games we allow rituals and imagery to become reasons themselves for playing. We allow our shared fantasies to forge a play community free of real-world limitations and bounded only by our visions.

Empowerment. *From the very start, New Games have been based on the principle of empowerment— giving the players control of and responsibility for their own play. It's really what we mean when we say that in New Games, we put the players first.*

Empowerment is perhaps best defined by the concept of the player/referee. If a game is to be for the benefit of the players, it should be conceived, led, and monitored by them as well. Likewise, the most effective way a leader can convey and effect the New Games attitude toward play is by participating as a player. This principle of empowering every participant as a player/referee can't be realized at the outset of every play session, but it is an ideal that we strive for whenever we get together to share New Games.

Some New Games empower the players by their structure. People to People starts with a caller who is frequently the leader of the group. As the game plays itself out, it places other players in the leader's role with the power to direct the game. In Get Down, the leader's role keeps expanding to include more players; by game's end, all of the players have made the transition from the periphery to the center of the game.

A game such as Samurai Warrior is also empowering by its nature. The warrior is placed in a position of control and power as she wields her sword. As the samurai, the game is her game. As we switch warriors, ownership of the game gets shared in turn by each player. Samurai Warrior is also empowering for the players who are targets, for it's up to them to referee themselves and indicate when they've made the wrong move.

A much more significant aspect of empowering is the way in which a game is presented and led. At the beginning of a play session and at other points during it, it may be necessary for the leader to assume a high-visibility role: organizing the group, deciding on the games to play, setting out the rules or safety considerations and seeing that they are followed and met. But leaders also look for opportunities to assume low-visibility roles, so that the players can take charge of the game. Generally, they do this by providing access to leadership of the game and by participating in the game, initially as a model for the players and ultimately as just another player/referee. A number of techniques for achieving this sort of leadership style are described in the essay "Tag, You're It!" Our objective is for the leaders to relinquish leadership to the players as everyone becomes a player/referee.

The empowerment principle is really the basis for attitudes we've discussed so far. In any of the soft-war games, the concept of caring restraint gives us, the participants, control of the challenge level of the game. In Behavior Modification, the two performers are dependent on the rest of us to keep the game fair by choosing appropriate actions, by giving good feedback, and even by offering hints if necessary. We're in control of the trust level of the game. It's obvious that the players are responsible for the safety of a rough game like Knock Your Socks Off. Fantasy in New Games allows all of us to construct a fantasy image, to free ourselves and our behavior in a safe context.

The most evident example of empowerment in New Games is the responsibility we take for creating the structure of our games. This final element of the New Games attitude—innovation—is perhaps the most exciting part of our approach to play. When we assume the power to make up the rules or change them, the game is truly ours.

40 **Innovation.** *We're always in the process of keeping New Games new. Whether we're playing a game described in one of our books, resurrecting an old childhood favorite, or brainstorming an entirely new game, we're continually looking for ways to make a game better, or maybe simply different. After all, New is our first name.*

Devising a game that is a bit different or strange can help us past old attitudes toward play. If we invite people to play softball, they'll each have longstanding opinions, positive or negative, about participating in the game. When we suggest a game of Clam Free, however, few of them will have any precon-ceptions or expectations about the game. From that starting point, we're free to play as we want to.

The freedom to innovate lets us change the rules if they're not meeting our needs. We could look at each game in this book—or at any game—and change it in terms of the concepts we've discussed. How could we make the challenges of a particular game more appropriate for particular players or groups? What could we add to increase the level of trust? How could a game be played more safely? How could its sense of fantasy and ritual be heightened? How could we modify the structure of a game, or the way in which it is led, to give the players more power or responsibility? Or how could we change a game just to make it fresh and new?

All of the games described in this book have evolved as we looked for answers to these kinds of questions. We continue to look for ways to play our favorite games differently and to seek new New Games to add to our roster. The real innovation in New Games, what really makes a game a New Game, is an attitude toward play that encourages everyone to benefit from the challenge of play and to share in the joys of play. It's an attitude that can work for these games or any game, as we carry the spirit of playfulness into our work and our lives. ■

Games for a Dozen

HIGH ACTIVITY
Triangle Tag
Swat
Frisbee Fakeout
Taffy Pull
Samurai Warrior
Ultimate Nerf
Star Wars

MEDIUM ACTIVITY
How Do You Do?
Snowblind
Group Juggling
Behavior Modification
Pile Up
Willow in the Wind
Pushpin Soccer

LOW ACTIVITY
Instant Replay
A What?
Name Train
Sightless Sculpture
Zen Clap
Killer
Mime Rhyme

Triangle Tag

Most New Games are played in circles, some are played in lines, and a few are played in squares. This game, then, is something of an oddity — it features the triangle. But let's not spend time pondering geometry. Let's divide into groups of four and play.

To start, three of us in each group hold hands in a triangle, facing each other. One of us volunteers to be the target. The fourth player stands outside the triangle as the chaser.

The object of the game is simple — the chaser tries to tag the target. However, the dynamics of the game are unique: The three players in the triangle all cooperate to protect the target by moving and shifting, and the target cannot be legally tagged on the hands or arms or from across the triangle.

If we want to make the game more challenging for the target protectors and a bit easier for the chaser, the people in the triangle can keep their hands on each other's shoulders. And if our players number a baker's dozen, we can have one chaser and four triangles, each with a target. Or two pentagons and three chasers. And while we're in this Euclidian frame of mind, why don't we start with triangles and invent a geometrical team game? ∎

Swat

There are always new uses for familiar play equipment. This game makes creative use of Boffers, those polyethylene swords that can make us all softwar swashbucklers or, in this case, can give a special flavor to a chase-and-tag game.

We stand in a circle, facing the center where we've placed a Boffer on top of a Frisbee or other marker. One player walks to the marker, picks up the Boffer, and commences to stalk the inside perimeter of the circle. Doing her best not to telegraph her intentions, she suddenly swats one of us with the Boffer (below the waist, please) and the action really begins.

The swatter must run back to the marker, lay the Boffer on it and return to the swatted person's place in the circle, and she must do this before her victim, the swattee, can recover the Boffer and tag her with it. If she succeeds, the swattee becomes the new swatter. However, if the swattee tags her, the chase starts again—for the swattee must drop the Boffer back on the marker and reach his original place in the circle before the swatter can recover the Boffer and tag him again.

This continues—with the Boffer always returned to the marker between swats—until one of these two players does manage to get back into place before being tagged. The person left holding the Boffer becomes the new swatter and begins stalking the circle for another victim.

This is a fast-paced game in which both reflexes and endurance come in handy. For that reason, Swat can be a great way to get our blood pumping and our eyes shining. There are some crucial responsibilities for us as players, however. We should take the usual safety precaution of playing

on a soft surface, and we should be considerate when we swat each other.

There are important psychological safety considerations too. In Swat, as in all games of tag, we should make sure that the same player isn't the swatter—isn't It—forever, getting more exhausted with each swat and becoming less and less likely ever to succeed in tagging another player. This self-governing is part of the caring restraint we use when we agree not to play too rough.

Swat is also a game that's ripe for creative variations. How about letting one of us in the circle switch into the swattee's original place while the action is proceeding? Or how about having two or more Boffers going at once, or playing the game blindfolded or in pairs? That Swat New Games are all about. ■

Frisbee Fakeout

The ubiquitous Frisbee, which the Wham-O Company would now rather have us call a "Frisbee brand flying disc," is without doubt the most inspired and playful creation to have emerged from the 1950s. If we start tossing one around with a few friends we're almost guaranteed to invent a New Game. Here's an eminently playable form of keep-away, flying-saucer style.

We lay out boundaries on a field so that we have three areas—two end zones with a slightly larger zone between them. We form two teams. One team stands in the central zone while the other team divides its players half in each end zone.

The end-zone team has possession of the Frisbee and tries to pass it from one end zone to the other without missing it or dropping it and without its being intercepted or knocked down by the other team. Everyone has to stay within the boundaries.

If the end-zone team fails to complete three attempted passes, or if the central-zone team intercepts a pass, the teams switch positions. The central-zone team sends half its players into each end zone and the end-zone players move to the middle section of the field to try to regain possession of the Frisbee. (The quicker this rotation is accomplished, the more exciting the game.)

We can devise elaborate scoring systems if we want to, or we can play just for the fun of making spectacular throws, trying for miraculous saves, and perfecting slick team fakeouts.

The size of the field has a great effect on the nature of this game, depending on the number of players and their skill level. The game seems to work best when the field is wider than it is long, but we can have a lot of fun using Frisbee Fakeout to experiment with boundary adjustment.

And let's keep our eyes open for more new ways to play with old toys. What happens to Frisbee Fakeout when we toss around another Wham-O creation and turn the game into Hula Hoopla? ■

Taffy Pull

The ingredients in this softwar recipe are all of the human variety. Amidst the tugging, some of our ideas about playing hard may get stretched too.

First, we make sure we're not wearing any sharp jewelry or belt buckles. Then we divide into teams—the taffy team and the taffy-pulling-machine team. The taffys all sit down and link hands, arms, and legs in a tangled mass of sweet humanity. They might want to decide what flavor they are and chant an appropriate confectionary cheer, like "Butterscotch, butterscotch." The taffys will need all the spirit and cohesiveness they can muster.

The rest of us are the taffy-pulling-machine team, and our job is to pull the taffy mass into human-sized bits. We might start with the parts of the taffy that appear to be the most stretchable, and firmly (but *gently*) tug at them until they come loose. Keep in mind that the best taffy is made by smooth stretches—if we yank too hard, the taffy will snap. And it's up to each bit of taffy to decide how much he wants to stay part of the mass. With these two important rules in mind, none of us should have to worry about getting hurt.

Our New Games taffy-pulling machine gets more powerful as it does its job. Each piece of taffy that gets separated from the mass joins the machine, until the last two die-hards are pulled apart. Then it's time for the original teams to switch roles for a new round of tasteful tugging, if everyone will stick with it. ∎

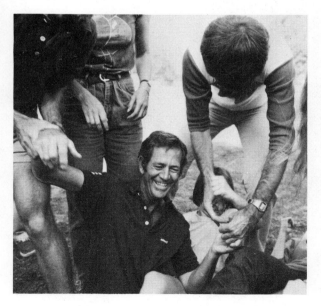

Samurai Warrior

Many of our New Game fantasies are aided by current book or movie crazes. This game was introduced at a New Games Trainers Conference in the Marin Headlands in California, but anyone who witnessed twelve prime-time hours of *Shōgun* bravado and sword swinging should already be primed for this bushido battle.

We can set up this game in a number of ways, as long as we have a samurai warrior armed with a samurai-sword Boffer and some human targets for him to swing at. The targets can form a circle around the samurai, or they can stand in a line in front of him or in two lines on either side of him, but they should always stand out of actual striking range of the Boffer.

When the samurai takes a swipe at the targets with his sword, his swing must be either high or low. If he swings high, all the targets have to duck. If he swings low, they have to jump. If the targets jump when they're supposed to duck, or vice versa, they're chopped in two and drop out of the game till the next round. It's up to the targets to referee themselves and know when they've been beheaded or defooted.

Really, though, this game is just an excuse for us to act out our oriental warfare fantasies. Surely no self-respecting samurai would stalk his targets without bowing to them, drawing his Boffer slowly from its scabbard, and embellishing each swing of the sword with intimidating cries. If his Japanese is a bit rusty, a simple "Eeeeaaah!" will do just fine to transport us back to feudal Japan.

Thank you, James Clavell. And, you see, television does have its value. Somewhere out there in TV land, we're sure someone's playing a game of Who Shot J.R.? ∎

Ultimate Nerf

Over the years, we've come up with a number of basic object-passing, goal-scoring team games that we call Ultimate. Stripped down to their essentials, such games involve two teams, a playing field with sidelines and a goal line at either end, and something that can be thrown, kicked or otherwise moved up and down the field. The object is for one team to move that something across the other team's goal line.

In Ultimate Nerf, for example, the something we move up and down the field is a Nerf ball—*Nerf* is the trademark of a soft foam ball made by Parker Brothers—and it starts with one team "kicking off" the ball to the opposing team, whose members can run anywhere on the field but cannot run with the ball—they can only catch and pass it. If a passed ball is dropped, thrown out of bounds, or intercepted, the other team immediately takes possession at that spot, and the direction of play shifts. Offensive and defensive players must stay about an arm's length apart.

Played just this way, Ultimate Nerf can provide a whole afternoon of fun. We can put lots of effort into elaborate team strategies or play it free form. We can decide how many goals constitute a win and play till one team vanquishes the other, or we can just play till we drop. We can also get to know a good deal about games and game change by experimenting with more elaborate variations.

Notice how we can alter the character of the game or adapt it to specific players by making the playing field larger or smaller, by varying how closely players may be guarded, by requiring a certain number of passes among teammates before a goal can be scored, by allowing players to take two steps with the ball as well as pass it, or by keeping score according to the quality of play rather than the quantity of goals.

If we're all reasonably proficient with flying discs, Ultimate Frisbee is a certified super Grade A New Game. We can play Ultimate games with anything that can be thrown and caught—paper airplanes, water balloons, or perhaps unconventional flying objects.

Or how about trying different field surfaces or shapes—snow? water? a figure-eight shaped field?—or different modes of locomotion—wheelchairs? slow motion? Or how about three teams?

We can have suspended baskets as goals and make a rule that we can run with the ball if we keep bouncing it. Or we can play on ice skates, passing a rubber disc from player to player by hitting it with wooden sticks, or on horseback with a ball and mallets. We can use helmets and shoulder pads and allow tackling. Or we can allow players to kick the ball but not to throw it or catch it.

As we experiment, we come to realize that, in general, the simpler we keep the game, the more people we can include who will enjoy playing it with us. And with that realization comes mastery of *the* ultimate game. ■

Star Wars

"Long ago, on a playground far, far away . . ."

Is it any wonder that the galactic consciousness that engulfed us a few years ago would give rise to a New Game? This death-star battle was first played at a New Games Training in Chapel Hill, North Carolina, during an invent-a-game session. It has Jedi knights, the Imperial Army, the rebel forces, death stars, and light sabers—what more could we need to fulfill our outer space fantasies?

We set up our galactic boundaries to create two large areas, each occupied by an army. A line separates the two areas and as many Nerf balls as we can gather (the more the better) are placed on this dividing line. These balls are death stars, which will soon be hurled through space.

One of us in each army is designated a Jedi knight—Luke of the rebels and Darth of the Empire. Each knight is armed with a light-saber Boffer, and each has a star base that is indicated by a Frisbee or other marker in his army's territory.

At an agreed-upon signal, the game begins. Both armies rush to the dividing line, gather as many death stars as they can, and begin hurling them at the opposing army. If one hits a player, the player is frozen immediately—imprisoned in a time warp. Only the player's Jedi knight can rescue her. He must leave his star base, hopping on one foot, and touch her with the light saber in order to bring her out of the time warp and back into the game. If a thrown ball is caught by the intended target, the thrower is frozen and must wait for help from his Jedi.

As long as the Jedi knights are at their star bases, they are safe. However, should one be hit by a death star while traveling to free a fellow teammate, he is frozen for good. Protection of the Jedi knights is therefore imperative. (As a variation, we can allow a frozen knight to pass the saber to another player, thus creating a new Luke or Darth.)

We realize we've only touched the surface of this rich fantasy. We can create special roles for Chewbacca, R2-D2, Yoda, or maybe one of the new characters that makes an appearance in the next *Star Wars* movie. In any case, as in all New Games, the Force is with *you*. ∎

How Do You Do?

Despite the fact that this game involves as mad a scramble as any circular chasing contest, its players never totally abandon their sense of etiquette.

We attend this game as party guests, standing in a circle and facing the center. One of us volunteers to be the host. He walks around the outside of the circle, behind our backs, and selects one player by tapping her on the shoulder. Now the formal pleasantries begin.

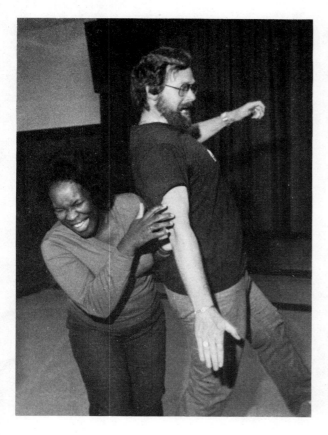

The host shakes the hand of the selected guest, introducing himself and inquiring, ever so solicitously, "How do you do?" She tells him her name and responds to his inquiry in her most genteel manner: "Fine, thank you!" But the host proves to be exceedingly gracious (or perhaps just hard of hearing), for he asks again, "How do you do?" whereupon the guest replies, again, "Fine, thank you!" The overly gracious host now asks for a *third* time, "How do you do?" all the while shaking the guest's hand. When she answers for the third time, "Fine, thank you!" all propriety is finally abandoned and the action begins.

The host dashes around the outside of the circle in the direction he was originally going, while the guest runs in the opposite direction. It's a contest to see who can get back to the starting place— home—first. However, when their paths cross somewhere on the other side of the circle, the host and the guest must stop, shake hands again, and go through the formalities three more times: "How do you do?" "Fine, thank you!" "How do you do?" "Fine, thank you!" "How do you do?" "Fine, thank you!" Then they continue on around the circle. Whoever gets beaten in the race home gets to host the party for the next round.

Can we add even more life to this madcap affair? How about specifying different forms of locomotion for the trip around the circle—hopping, skipping, or side-stepping, perhaps. Or how about making the host and the guest get around the circle walking backward or with their eyes closed? Or we could exchange pleasantries and race around the circle in pairs, just to add to the formal frenzy. ∎

Snowblind

This game was invented during a New Games training session in Cincinnati, using the invent-a-game grid described on page 102. The seven elements given were snow, tag, chain, Boffers, eyes closed, It/not It, and chanting. This game was the result. (Notice how the prescribed environment—snow—was incorporated into the fantasy rather than taken literally.)

We begin by establishing boundaries and choosing one player to be the snowman. He arms himself with a Boffer, and because he is snowblind, he must keep his eyes closed. The rest of us crouch on the ground, eyes open, and wait for the snowman to start the action by chanting, "Snowman, snowman, all in white, blinding everyone in sight!" While he chants, we can run around in bounds, but we must return to a stationary crouching position by the time the chant ends.

Now it's the snowman's turn to move around while we remain in our positions and repeat his chant, in unison. Still snowblind, of course, the snowman tries to tag one of us with the Boffer, guided only by sound. When he succeeds, the tagged player

becomes snowblind, too, and she must join forces with the snowman, who gives the Boffer to her and stands behind her with his hands on her hips. Then they both close their eyes and say the chant while the rest of us run for safety again. Then we chant while the two-person snowman tries to locate and tag us.

As the game continues, round by round, the snowman grows into a long chain of people. Each newly tagged player joins the snowman at the head of the chain, and everyone in the snowman chain must keep his eyes closed. (A referee can make sure the snowman chain doesn't wander off in a blizzard.) The last round of the game will pit a long string of snowblind players against a single survivor.

Thank you, Cincinnati folks, for a great New Game. ■

Group Juggling

Fellow bumblers, fear no more! There is a way to juggle that's as much fun as the traditional method and a lot less work. We just combine a dozen or so aspiring jugglers and a game of catch.

We stand in a circle, facing the center, with our hands raised in the air. Starting with one ball, we catch it and throw it, establishing a pattern. One of us tosses the ball to someone on the other side of the circle, say, and she tosses it to a third person who tosses it to a fourth and so on, until everyone has tossed and caught the ball once. (We each drop our hands when we've had a turn.) The last catcher tosses the ball back to the player who started the pattern, and we all run through the sequence again, for practice. Now the real juggling can begin.

With one ball on its way around the circle, we add another, so that we have two balls in the air following the catch-and-toss pattern. Now we add another ball, and by this time we should be watching carefully for midair collisions, trying to toss the ball so that the intended receiver can catch it, and perhaps calling out the names of the receivers as we toss the ball to them. We should remember that this is a cooperative venture: We want to keep as many balls in the air as we can, but if one drops, we should just pick it up and keep the pattern going.

We can continue to add balls, or we can reverse the balls' direction and send them through the pattern in opposite order. How about one ball going in one direction and another one going in the opposite direction simultaneously? We can keep making the game more challenging as we get better at it.

You're wondering about those Hula-Hoops in the photo? No, you don't need them for this game, but someone just happened to bring a passel of hoops to the beach, and we couldn't resist thinking up things to do with them. Group Hoop was an instant success. ■

Behavior Modification

With due acknowledgement to B. F. Skinner, we proudly present this delightful exercise in positive reinforcement.

Two of us are selected as the subjects of this not-so-serious scientific pursuit and are briefly excused from the rest of the group. Once the subjects are out of range, the rest of us decide on a pose or an action we want the subjects to copy. It might be standing on one leg and holding hands, or linking elbows and bending over, or performing a tandem push-up. It's important that the pose be specific enough to be identifiable, but not too difficult or detailed. (Standing pigeon-toed with third and fourth fingers crossed while looking over your left shoulder and whistling "Home on the Range," for instance, is too detailed!)

Once we all know the exact pose, the two subjects are called back and they attempt to replicate it. They try various moves and check for our response. We register how close they are to the desired pose by clapping loudly or softly, or by cheering or booing, or by making a high or low hum. As we all continue to signal "hot" or "cold," the subjects should get the picture.

The subjects' best strategy is to try all sorts of moves until they get a rise out of the group. Then they should hold everything until they can isolate which of their moves is part of the desired position. When the two subjects do hit upon the right pose, let's offer them the ultimate positive reinforcement of a standing ovation, and perhaps a graduate degree in human behavior. ∎

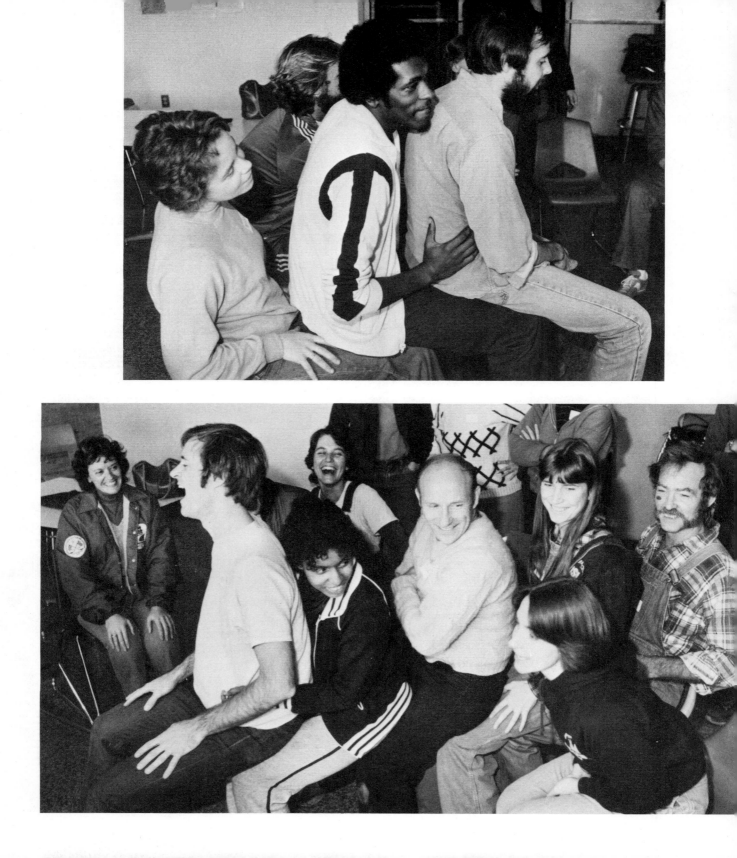

Pile Up

In this chair-switching game, everyone is assured of a place to sit, although there's no reserved seating and no guarantee of single occupancy.

We start with each person sitting on a chair in a circle, one person to a seat. Now we each pose questions to the group that can be answered yes or no, such as "Are you left-handed?" "Were you born west of the Mississippi?" "Do you have a sister?" "Do you prefer cantaloupe to honeydew?"

Whoever answers a question yes moves one chair to the right. Whoever answers no stays in his seat. When a player moves over to a chair that's already occupied, she sits on the lap of the occupant.

We keep asking questions until all of us are piled on the same chair. Accomplishing this aggregation via interrogation can be quite a challenge if we make the rule that no questions can be based on qualities that are visible, which would make a question like "Do you have blue eyes?" illegal. But if there are not too many of us and if we play some shrewd hunches and devise creative queries, we should eventually be able to get ourselves piled up and get to know each other a little better in the process.

What? No chairs handy? No reason not to play. This game can be played on the floor, grass, sand, in the pool (shallow end), wherever. We simply sit with our legs apart in a V position and pile up! When the game's over, we're all set for group back rubs. ■

Willow in the Wind

Imagine a warm summer night. Crickets are chirping, and graceful willows are swaying in a gentle, perfumed breeze. If we can imagine it, we can be there, with this New Games experience that cradles each of us in caring, supportive hands.

We form a small circle of about eight players standing shoulder to shoulder and facing the center of the circle with hands held at chest height, palms forward. Each of us should have one foot slightly behind the other for good balance. We've just transformed ourselves into a summer breeze, and now all we need is a volunteer to be the willow.

The willow stands in the center of the circle with her feet together, her arms crossed over her chest, and her eyes closed. Keeping her feet stationary and her body straight but relaxed, she lets herself go, swaying from side to side, forward and back. Those of us in the circle support her with gentle pushes of our palms and provide summer-breeze sound effects. We should make sure that there are at least two people supporting the willow at all times and that our gentle breeze does not become a howling hurricane.

In turn, each of us gets to be the willow in the wind, swaying to and fro, caressed by the breeze. This is a trust game. The player who is the willow gets the opportunity to trust the other players completely, and those of us who are the breeze get to feel the trust the willow has placed in us. ∎

Pushpin Soccer

Sometimes we have to take advantage of play opportunities wherever and whenever they arise. We tried this game on a big yellow school bus en route to a New Games Festival, and though it didn't do much for our relationship with the bus driver, we did have a rousing good time.

We divided into two teams, evenly dispersed among the rows of seats on the bus, and blew up a bunch of balloons. At the front of the bus, armed with a pushpin, stood team A's goalie, and team B's goalie, similarly armed, took command of the rear seat. The object was for each team to swat a balloon toward its own goalie, who would pop it. Everyone had to stay seated and be wary of direct contact with pushpins.

We rapidly made two discoveries. First, our F.I. (Fun Intensity) level increased almost without limit in direct proportion to the number of balloons we had going at the same time. Second, after Nancy started celebrating goals by banging on the roof of the bus, team A became almost unbeatable.

Alternative seating arrangements and environments are left to your creative whim. ∎

Instant Replay

Ever get the feeling that all those spectacular touchdown passes we see over and over on the tube each week are cut from the same piece of film? The instant replays in this game are not only guaranteed to be unique, they also provide a perfect way for us to introduce ourselves—again and again and again.

Let's all stand in a circle, facing each other. One of us starts by moving a few steps into the center and announcing his name while performing whatever movements and gestures he chooses. For instance, he might skip into the center and perform a grand sweeping wave of his hand, proclaiming to all, "Fred!" (assuming that's his name, of course) and then skip back to his place in the circle. That's the signal for everyone else to do *exactly* as he did, in unison, mimicking him in both deed and word as closely as possible.

Next, it's Sarah's turn. Maybe she slithers into the center and hisses a serpentine "Sssssarah!" The rest of us then get to be snakelike Sarahs too. We proceed around the circle, each of us getting a turn to announce himself in his own way and to see himself in multiple instant replay.

The announcements can convey occupations or secret selves, or they can have no particular meaning at all. With or without categories, the first player can get things rolling in the right spirit by setting a creatively silly example. But everyone should choose motions that everyone else will be able to repeat; in other words, no two-and-a-half gainers with a slipped disc (also known as the Not Nadia Rule).

The best part of this game is that there's no such thing as a second-rate performance. If you think you're going to play it safe by timidly trudging into the circle and muttering, "Marie," just wait until you see yourself on instant replay. ■

A What?

The name of this game is A What? A What?? A What?! And if that's confusing, just wait until we start playing. In this game, no one ever knows exactly *what* is happening.

We stand in a circle, facing the center. One of us starts the action by taking a ball (any object will do) and handing it to the person on his right, saying, "This is a banana." The person who now holds the ball is evidently already confused, because she inquires, "A what??" The first player repeats, "A banana!"

Person number two, her confusion temporarily cleared up, hands the ball to the person on her right and says, "This is a banana." Now person number three is confused. "A what???" he asks of number two. She then turns back to number one and asks again, "A what??" "A banana!" he says. Whereupon number two turns back to three and confirms it. "A banana!!" she says. Now that number three is enlightened, he can hand the ball he's been holding to the person on his right, number four, and say, "This is a banana." And when number four asks, "A what????" the whole sequence gets played back to number one: "A what???" "A what??" "A banana!" "A banana!!" "A banana!!!"

While number four starts the process all over again with number five, number one takes another ball, hands it to the person on his *left*, and says, "This is a pineapple." "A what??" And the pineapple takes off to the left. By the time the two balls collide somewhere in the circle, who'll be able to say for sure what's what?

When we become pros at this game, we can add more balls to the fruit bowl. Maybe a pomegranate. A what? ■

Name Train

Every player is a superstar in New Games, and here's a way to make sure that each of us receives an ovation to match that status.

We stand in a circle, facing the center, and one player volunteers to be the locomotive. If he's a genuine railroad buff, he'll take a few chugs around the circle, piston-driving with his arms, choo-chooing, and maybe letting blast with a steam whistle or two. (No diesels in this game.)

The locomotive stops and exchanges introductions with one of us in the circle: "Hi, I'm Bob." "Hello, I'm Mary." Upon learning the person's name, Bob the locomotive breaks into a semaphore-style cheer, alternately raising his arms and extending his legs while chanting the person's name: "Mary! Mary! Mary, Mary, Mary!"

After Mary has been hailed, Bob the locomotive turns around, Mary places her hands on his hips as a caboose, and the two of them chug across the circle to find another person to introduce themselves to. "Hi, I'm Gregory," says the chosen player. Bob repeats Gregory's name; then Mary repeats it, and then they both break into semaphoric euphoria, chanting, "Gregory! Gregory! Gregory, Gregory, Gregory!" Following Gregory's chant, Mary becomes the locomotive, Bob puts his hands on her waist, and Gregory joins the train as the new caboose, and they all chug off to acquire another car.

We continue adding cars to the train, cheering everyone by name as we go along. We might even split into two or more trains (depending on the number of players) before each of us has been duly celebrated and added to the *New Games Express*. What's next? A game of Loose Caboose, of course. ∎

Sightless Sculpture

We don't need a studio with a northern exposure to produce works of art in this game. Sometimes our most inspired moments arise when we're in the dark.

We divide into groups of three. In each group, one player is the artist, one the model, and the third a lump of clay. The artist and the clay close their eyes while the model (who can keep his eyes open) strikes a fanciful pose. The more detailed and creative the pose, the better. It should, however, be one that can comfortably be held for about five minutes.

Now it's time for the artist and the clay, eyes still closed, to demonstrate their duplicative dexterity. The artist gently gropes the model to discover his exact pose and then molds the clay into an identical statue. When the artist thinks his creation is perfect, he and the new statue can open their eyes and submit the sculpture to the scrutiny of the rest of us, art critics all.

How about trying some supersized group sightless sculptures using a multitude of models, colossal clumps of clay, and an army of artists? ■

Zen Clap

We may not get to hear the sound of one hand clapping during this game, but we're likely to encounter just about every other distraction in this test of concentration and presence of mind.

We all sit in a circle, facing each other. One of us starts the action by placing either hand, with fingers extended, on top of her head, saying, "Yin."

Whoever goes next depends on which way the starter's fingers are pointing. If she used her left hand, her fingers would be pointing to the person in the circle to her right, and so that person would go next. If she used her right hand, her fingers would point to the left, and so the person to the left of the starter would continue the game.

What does that next person do? She places either hand, with fingers extended, under her chin and says, "Yang." And whichever way her fingers are pointing, left or right, indicates who in the circle goes next.

Now the third player has the best part of all. She performs a one-handed clap by pointing her fingertips toward anyone else in the circle while saying nothing at all. (That's the sound of the well-known Zen clap, as far as we know.) Whichever way her fingertips point indicates a new starter, who gets the whole process rolling again by placing one hand on top of his head and saying, "Yin." The game continues—"Yin!" "Yang!" silent clap—at as rapid a pace as possible, until some distracted soul makes the wrong motion, says the wrong word, or goes out of turn.

For such a transgression, the daydreamer is banished from the circle of Zen masters. However, in true New Games style, he gets to remain in the game, as a satori heckler. In this role, he's allowed to stand just outside the circle and do or say anything (short of touching a player or blocking her vision) to try to make someone else miss. Whoever goofs joins the ranks of the hecklers, until there are just a few Zen masters trying to stay centered amidst the confusion. When there are only three masters left, it's time for a new round. But first ask them, "Who has won the game before it starts?" ∎

Killer

This game is a classic whodunit. It seems that there's a sneaky killer operating in our midst. How do we know? We're being bumped off one by one! It's up to all of us to give our best Miss Marple and Hercule Poirot performances and force the villain to confess before we're all wiped out.

We start by assembling a cast of characters for our mystery and selecting the killer. We can choose pieces of paper, one of which is marked with a cross to signify the killer, or we can close our eyes, place our thumbs together and have someone who is not playing choose the killer by squeezing one set of thumbs. Once we have a killer, it's simply a matter of whether he will murder us all before being caught in the act.

The killer's *modus operandi* is exceptionally clandestine—a wink of the eye directed at an intended victim does the trick. As the game gets underway, we mingle, exchanging furtive glances. If any of us is winked at, he's just been murdered.

The victim then has the opportunity to do his favorite death scene. Since it's important that the whole group knows who has been eliminated, he's encouraged to crumple, stagger, and gasp as part of the dying act. To keep the killer's identity from being too obvious, though, there should be a three- to five-second delay between the wink and the death throes.

For the survivors, the situation is becoming more grim by the moment. Our companions are dropping all around us. We'd better discover the murderer before we, too, are eliminated from the game in a wink. What's our deductive method?

If one of us suspects the killer's identity, she says, "I have an accusation!" However, a single accusation does not suffice in this game; unless someone else says, "I second the accusation," we've got to continue playing.

If another suspicious soul does second, the two accusers count to three and point to the player they each think is the perpetrator—no conferences allowed. If they both point to a suspect who's innocent, or if they both point to different suspects (even if one of those suspects *is* guilty), they're dead on the spot because of inept detective work. If, however, they both point to the true killer, he makes a complete and remorseful confession, and the crime of the century is solved.

Killer provides marvelous opportunities for creative variations, supplemental rules, and devious strategies. In Classic Killer, for example, we don't mingle. Instead, we sit in a circle so everyone has a clear view of everyone else while our eyes jump and dart in anticipation of the fatal wink. Marathon Killer, in which we set up the game and then go about our business, is a great game for adding suspense and drama to an evening gathering or weekend event. In Killer Plague, a murdered victim can take others to the grave with him if he tags them as he dies. In all forms of Killer, beware of the setup or double cross. What happens if the prime suspect seconds an accusation?

If all this murderous activity is offensive, we can change the fantasy and play Lover, with romantic swoons instead of death throes. But if we can accept softwar, what's wrong with a little soft crime? ∎

Mime Rhyme

Here's a chance to try out your skill as a mime and play a New Game too. No need to have studied with Marcel Marceau—a healthy imagination will serve you as well as expert training.

We gather in a comfortable group. (What? No circle?) One of us reveals that he's thinking of a word and it rhymes with—*deep*, for example. The rest of us try to figure out the chosen word, testing our guesses by acting them out in pantomime.

For instance, one of us closes his eyes and rests his head on his hands, only to be told by the person who selected the word, "No, it's not *sleep*." Other players try crawling sneakily and jumping high in the air, but the answer isn't *creep* or *leap*. Other possible guesses to mime: honking a horn, wiping away imaginary tears, driving a vehicle that can take on bumpy roads, or peering through a tiny hole.

Well, there *are* still several more words to guess and a thousand more rhymes to mime. ∎

Tag, You're It!

Sooner or later (sooner, we hope), you'll want to share New Games with your family, friends, coworkers, students, campers, or play group. Whether you're making a formal presentation or simply taking part in a casual get-together, you'll probably feel added responsibilities and challenges in your role of leading New Games.

In the following pages, we'll offer some practical suggestions gleaned from the many trainings, workshops, and festivals we've conducted, with the hope that they might make your own play session more successful and fun. We can't say exactly how you should proceed with your players—after all, no two groups are the same. Your best guide will be to keep in mind the New Games attitude toward play and to apply it to the needs and tastes of the people with whom you're playing.

Most importantly, be sure to draw upon the resources of your players and to add a healthy dose of your own personality and creativity. In no time, you'll find yourself part of a truly playful community.

Getting Started. *For some of us, getting a group into play is the most challenging part of a New Games session. Before plunging in, try to get a sense of the group you'll be playing with. How are they dressed? What kind of physical shape are they in? Does the group include children and adults? Does everybody seem to know each other? Have they already begun to play or interact? Don't worry if the group doesn't conform to your expectations. (Better yet, try not to have any expectations.) Start with the group as it is and go on from there.*

Let's say you're facing a ready-made group assembled just to play New Games with you. Introduce yourself and invite everyone to join you in a game. Let everyone know that you're extending an open invitation—that is, they are all welcome to play, but they don't have to play. Both your words and gestures should assure them that the game is going to be fun.

To start, you'll want a game that gets the whole group involved right away. Even if everyone is wearing gym suits and sneakers, start slowly with an interactive game that's not too strenuous. Some good starting games for a ready-made group might be People to People, Everybody's It, Octopus, or Group Juggling. The appropriateness of the first game depends as much on how it is presented and led as it does on which particular game is chosen.

From your first game, you should get an even better sense of the players. Be prepared to reassess your judgment about their playfulness. Remember not to expect them to take too big a risk—either physically or psychologically—too quickly.

If you arrive at the play site ahead of time and the players wander in, begin the session gradually. Don't wait, aloof from the group, until you think enough people have arrived. Establish relationships with

the individual players right away. Introduce yourself, find out about them. Start tossing around some Frisbees or Nerf balls. Turn that into a game of Group Juggling and you've got the games underway.

Keep an eye out for new arrivals and include them in the game, or switch to a new game as the number of players increases. The key to the slow-arrival situation is to continually extend an open and welcoming invitation to new players. Build the group's playful spirit gradually, and establish yourself as a player as well as the leader right from the start.

A third typical starting situation is the festival setting, in which there may be hundreds of people assembled in a very informal way. They may have come with some expectation that New Games will be played, or they may be there for some other event and you are undertaking to include New Games as part of the activities. This situation may at first seem overwhelming—all those people and no one's attention focused on you. How can you get everyone involved?

The best approach is to start small. Go up to someone and ask them if they want to play a game. Try to invite them in the same playful and encouraging way you approached the other situations. You might have to coax them a bit. ("It's fun, give it a try.") Try some one-on-one games, such as Commons, Quick Draw, Me Switch, Butt Off, Toe Fencing, or Last Detail.

Once you've got one person involved in a game, the next step is to add another player. Find a passer-by and suggest that your first player teach the second one the game you've been playing. Meanwhile, find a third person and start a game with her. Now you've got four people involved, enough for Triangle Tag or Samurai Warrior. If another leader has been engaged in this process, too, you can join forces and have eight players. That's enough for a game of Swat, Zen Clap, or A What? Invite a few more people and you'll have enough for Name

Train, Group Juggling, or How Do You Do?

You can also try a more direct approach in a festival setting, especially if you're working with two or three other leaders. Each of you grabs hands with two likely players. Have them join hands and then move the chain into a circle and start with a game like Instant Replay. The key to making New Games work in a festival setting is to assemble a "critical mass" of players and keep the play energy concentrated and focused.

Whatever the situation, begin with games that provide easy access and that have few rules, games that can be ended quickly so a transition can be made to a new game. Let the players stretch their bodies and their feelings slowly at first. As a leader, be inviting, clear, and maybe a bit silly. Model the style of play you want to encourage. Most important, have in mind a few starters that are likely to fit the group you'll be facing. Make them games that you enjoy playing and presenting, games that you feel confident and comfortable with. From them, you'll be able to choose a first game that's just right.

Presenting. *The way you present your games will greatly affect the way they'll be played. Whether you're facing one person or a crowd, the same advice applies: Explain the game's structure and rules as clearly and simply as possible, and do it in a style that encourages participation, playfulness, and fun.*

Begin by describing the game in a general way. Start with its name and the fantasy or imagery it employs, and explain the game's object, or fit it into a familiar game category. ("Let's play Star Wars. It's a kind of dodge ball with Jedi knights, light sabers and death stars.") Combine the description with demonstration—people will understand the rules much better if they can see the action. For example, in Elephant/Palm Tree/ Monkey, set up the game formation, a circle, and help three players arrange themselves in the poses the game requires.

Make sure everyone can see and hear you. Stand at the edge rather than in the center of a circle so that your back is not to anyone. With some games, people won't be able to hear you if you set up the game formation, so you'll have to separate the description from the demonstration. ("We're going to play

a game called Lemonade, and you'll be in two teams on either side of this line, but let me explain part of the game before we get into teams.")

When you've described and demonstrated the game, ask for questions to make sure that everyone has understood. If a particular question suggests an interesting variation, you might use it as an opportunity to empower the players, to let the group take charge of the game. ("That's an interesting suggestion; do we want to try playing that way?") Don't get caught up in involved questions; many times people will get the hang of a game quickly once they begin playing.

If there are two or more leaders working as a team at the play session, there should be an agreement as to who is presenting a particular game. Two leaders can operate well together if one assumes the high-visibility role of explaining the game while the other takes a low-visibility role—setting up boundaries, getting people into formation, and participating as a player in demonstrations.

Throughout the presentation, it's important to extend an invitation to

play. Say "Let's try . . ." instead of "You're going to . . ." Always give people choices. Ask for volunteers when you need someone to play a special role in a game or to start the action. If you don't get a volunteer, then take the role on yourself or ask a fellow leader.

If a game involves a special form of action, such as the bent-over position in Jamaquack or the dramatic deaths in Killer, have everyone practice before the game starts. They'll get a chance to overcome whatever uneasiness they might have at doing something flamboyant or silly, and when the game gets underway, everyone will put much more spirit into it.

Some games involve a fair amount of psychological risk taking. Name Train and Instant Replay, which spotlight one player, are good examples. If, as the leader, you're able to demonstrate the game with appropriately outrageous or foolish words and actions, you can serve as a model, encouraging all the players to quickly cast aside their inhibitions and join you. But watch out that you're not too silly for the group, or you might lose them rather than encourage them.

If a game involves physical risks, make sure that you have the full

attention of the group as you explain safety considerations. Having the group fan out to check the playing area for hazards is more than simply an expedient method of examining a large area quickly; it is an excellent way to start building safety awareness among all the players.

Before a physically active game, point out any special qualities of the group's physical makeup that require special safety precautions. A good way to highlight safety needs is to put them in personal terms. ("I don't want to get hurt in this game, so let's make sure that we all . . .") When appropriate, explain the caring-restraint principle and the Stop Rule described in the section on safety in the essay "Tag, You're It!" Another method

of keeping a game safe is to point out the way that strategy rather than force can win it. This can keep it from becoming a purely physical contest.

When presenting games, always look for opportunities to make the game fantasy or imagery come alive. Set up the fantasy by having everyone imagine the setting for the game. ("This parachute is a great big swamp.") Encourage people to let go of the real world and really be the character of the game, whether it's a snowman, a piece of taffy, or a balloon, by convincingly demonstrating the role yourself. The freer you are, the freer the other players will be.

Most importantly, be yourself. Develop your own style of presentation. As we've said, it's the aspect of presenting a game that most determines how everyone will play it. The way you demonstrate how the swatter stalks the circle in Swat will set the mood for the game. The first time you say, "Hey, there! You're a real cool cat" in Get Down, you'll be modeling the jive talk for the subsequent rounds.

Whatever your presentation style, don't take yourself or the game too seriously. A genuine fun-loving spirit is very contagious. Keep your sense of humor and your enthusiasm for the games you present, and you'll find that everyone will play them with humor and enthusiasm too.

90   **Choosing Sides.** *In New Games, dividing into teams is never a traumatic experience for a player, because he never has to worry that he'll be the last chosen. Instead, New Games makes choosing sides a game in itself.*

One great choosing-sides game is called Ducks and Cows. All the players close their eyes, and the leader whispers the word duck or cow to each player. (Players can raise their hands until they've received a barnyard identity.) When everyone has been deemed either a duck or a cow, the members of each species get together to form one team. But since their eyes are closed, the only means by which they can locate their teammates is boisterous and spirited quacking or mooing, as the case may be. By the time the two groups have formed, everyone will be ready for a playful game of Lemonade, Giants/Elves/Wizards, or Frisbee Fakeout.

Another choosing-sides game is called Mingle. Everyone does just that, moving about randomly, shaking hands, introducing themselves, making small talk. When the leader yells, "Teams" or "Partners,"

players group with the person or people nearest them, and you've got instant teams. (You can get different team sizes by calling out a number. For Triangle Tag, you'd yell, "Teams of four.")

Try choosing sides playing Vowels. Everyone sings the first vowel of his name. When the a's, e's, i's, o's, and u's are gathered and crooning together, you'll have five teams to mix and match according to the needs of the game.

Try playing Data Processing as a way of dividing into teams. Some categories to consider: food preferences (mustard vs. catsup, vanilla vs. chocolate); family relationships (first child vs. middle child vs. last child, people with sisters vs. people with brothers vs. people with both); apparel (watch wearers vs. watchless, dark shirts vs. light shirts). It might prove interesting to see how a team of vanilla lovers or watch wearers conduct's itself in a particular game.

There are also a number of odd physical traits that can serve to divide people into teams. Have everyone hop on one foot and then play the lefties against the righties. Have them clasp their hands and then divide according to which thumb, left or right, is on top. Have them look at their nails. Those who kept their hands flat with their palms down can play against those who curled their fingers with their palms up. Whatever categories you choose, don't pass up the opportunity to get each team chanting their team name or identity. ("Palms up!" "Palms up!")

By making choosing sides a playful experience in itself, you can set the mood for the game to follow and let everyone know that whichever team wins, what's important is that everyone has fun playing.

Playing/Refereeing. *Once a game gets underway, you should play too—that's the model of the player/referee. By joining the action, you minimize the distinction between players and leaders, and that's the goal of New Games. But you should also keep an eye on how the game's proceeding and be prepared to make adjustments in the game or guide the group (moving back into a higher-visibility leadership role, if necessary) if you spot ways to reinforce the New Games attitude toward play.*

In a game such as Giants/Elves/ Wizards, you may notice that some players are running as fast as they can to try to tag their opponents or avoid being tagged. Other players might be content to jog back to the goal. If you suggest that the speedy runners line up toward the middle of each line and the joggers at the ends, the game will be challenging and more fun for all of the players, regardless of their ability or mood on that particular day. Lining up that way may prevent injuries as well.

You may want to suggest an actual modification of the game to maintain or create a balance in the level of challenge. You could add a

fourth character to Elephant/Palm Tree/Monkey, or change the boundaries or the number of misses allowed in Frisbee Fakeout. You could add more balls to Monarch. In general, make just one change at a time. And read on— adapting games in this manner is dealt with in more detail later.

Make sure that a game doesn't become too goal oriented. The misses in Group Juggling are a good opportunity to add humor to the game. ("Primal screams are allowed.") In Behavior Modification, there's ample opportunity for creative cheating in the form of hints. Don't feel the need to play elimination games such as Octopus down to the last survivor.

Make sure that everyone has the opportunity to play different roles in a game so that some people don't dominate; but otherwise leave it up to the players or the game itself to determine who will be It next. Often, whoever is tagged is It; in games where this is not the case, a pattern will likely evolve in which the last person doing such and such starts the new round. To underline the availability of choices, let everyone know that the pattern can be broken.

Although oftentimes you might want to let a game run its course to

see where the players take it, you should always remain aware of the physical safety of a game. Sometimes you'll spot a potential hazard as the game gets underway. For instance, in Quick Lineup, you might want to establish that each player has to get back in line without touching another player. If a game is becoming dangerously rough, feel free to step in and remind the players of the purpose of playing. Make use of the game spirit being generated to bring the situation to light. ("Hey, this game of Octopus is turning into Calamari Crunch!") Sometimes merely breaking the physical momentum of a game for a moment will bring everyone back to a safety awareness.

As you play, encourage the make-believe and imagery in a game. In Human Compressor, have the players describe what color and shape balloons they are. In Knight's Move, have each player tell what sort of chess piece he is—carved ivory, sculpted clay, carved stone. The games will come to life. Add ritual noise or chanting wherever possible. In Wink, have all the players slap the ground as they count out the time limit for the contest between the winkee and his partner. In Elbow Tag, have the runner shout, "Go!" when she links elbows with a pair. This will signal the new runner to take off; it will also add noise to the game and keep everyone attentive and enthusiastic.

Group huddles are a great way of building a shared play energy and adding to the excitement of play. In Lemonade, encourage cheering and team camaraderie as the team huddles to decide on the next occupation. Good-natured taunting of the other team is a major aspect of this game. ("What's your trade? Nah-nah-nah-nah-nah!") The fact that the composition of the teams changes with each round only serves to highlight the realization that the embellished team rivalry is just for fun.

Throughout the play session, look for opportunities to empower the players to take charge of and responsibility for their games. Since you've started the session as the leader, players will naturally appeal to you for rules interpretations. Turn the decision back to them. ("Can he run as soon as he's tagged?" "What do you think?") If someone makes a suggestion for a variation ("Maybe we need more balls in the game"), don't let it slide by. Involve the group in changing the rules.

The notion of self-refereeing and being a player/referee is foreign to most players. Let it be known that they're all taking care of one another. Remind players that safety is the responsibility of each player.

Once the game is underway, a low-visibility leadership role is best. You'll probably continue to function as the leader, but there's no need to make everyone acknowledge that you're in charge. Don't just step in and announce a new game, for example. Let a game run its course. If it appears to be sagging, give the players an option. ("Shall we play another round, or a new game?")

The New Games model emphasizes shared leadership, but it's usually not enough merely to step back and hope that other group members will take over. Many times, a blanket permission for anyone or everyone in the group to become the leader is not effective. Individual invitations to lead games are often needed. Look for players who might be ready or willing to present games and invite them to present the next game. And don't pass up the opportunity to ask players to suggest games of their own. That's the best way to learn a new New Game.

Creating a Repertoire. *If you're going to be leading New Games for the first time, don't try to memorize all the games in this book and be prepared to play them. You will be much better off with a list of, say, twelve games that you know well and feel confident about than you will be with a list of sixty games you're not able to lead. Of your twelve, you'll probably only need six—half a dozen games that are thoroughly played and enjoyed will easily comprise a play session lasting more than an hour, and that's a long time if you're really involved in playing.*

As you create your repertoire, think of the qualities of each game. Some games involve a high level of physical activity; others permit the players to take it easy. Softwar games allow players to be aggressive. Trust games focus on the need for mutual support in a play community. Some games have as their main element creative play—they allow players to act out fantasy roles or require that players think of ways to mentally stump their opponents. Many, many New Games combine these elements.

In your games list, you want a mix of game types, a mix of elements. If you take time to analyze a game's qualities and potential qualities (remember that a game can be greatly affected by the way it is presented and led), you'll be able to use games creatively to pace your play sessions.

One of the main things to think about as you pace a play session is its physical activity level. You want to keep it matched with the abilities of the players, using high-activity games to pick up the group spirit and low-activity games to give players time to catch their breath or rest. All the while you can be building the level of trust and risk taking within the group. Generally, you want to establish a trusting relationship among the players before you play games that involve special safety concerns, close body contact, or individual initiative and creative expression.

Another factor to consider is group focus. Games that are played in a circular formation create an awareness of the play group as a whole. Games played in opposing lines or as field contests have more random action and let the focus become fragmented. Free-form activities generate the most individual expression but maintain the weakest ties among the players. By choosing particular games, you can let up on the level of group focus if the session is becoming too ordered and stagnant, or you can

use the more formally structured games to keep the group together. For the last game, you'll probably want to bring closure to the session with a game such as Vortex, Get Down, or the Lap Game, which was included in The New Games Book.

It is helpful to have a list of games written out and available to check during the session. While a game is underway, take a look at your list and arrive at some idea of what game you want to try next. When a game suddenly comes to a halt and the players look at you expectantly, you'll be prepared.

You may want to organize the games on your list by activity level and number of players, as we've done on page 190, marking games that emphasize special qualities of softwar, trust, or creative play. You may want to flag low-risk games that are good for openers or sure-fire games that you especially like or feel confident in leading. Some people find it useful to group games into sets of six to ten games that present a good progression of activities and qualities. As your session proceeds, you can follow the set progression that you've thought out in advance, or improvise by jumping ahead in the set or mixing games from different sets.

All of these may be helpful suggestions in planning your play

sessions, but don't feel that you have to have a degree in games engineering to play New Games. There's no right order in which to play New Games and no perfect next game. The most important skill you can bring to your play session is sensitivity. If you try to stay aware of how your group wants to play, your repertoire for the session will naturally take shape.

If you're interested in building your games repertoire, you might try keeping one list of games that you've led before and are familiar with, and another list of games you've never played. At each session, experiment by playing one of your old favorites and modify it during the course of the game, or play a game you've never tried, or try one suggested by another player. Your games list will stay vital while your repertoire grows.

Using Equipment. We're fond of saying that you don't need equipment to play New Games, and it's really true. Fifty of the games in this book require nothing more than smiling people ready to play. For Frisbee Fakeout, Ultimate Nerf, and Monarch, you'll need a ball or disc to toss around (a few more balls for Group Juggling). Roll up a newspaper to substitute for a Boffer and you're set for Swat, Samurai Warrior, and Star Wars. If you're dying to play Pushpin Soccer, you'll need to find a package of balloons and a couple of pins. And there you have fifty-eight games to play before you have to track down an Earthball or a parachute.

If you do collect some playthings, you can use them to add excitement to the games, especially at the beginning of a session when you want to get people involved. Attractive or unusual equipment can help motivate people to play. If it's too attractive or unusual, however, much of the play energy can get diverted to the equipment, rather than being focused on the players and the game. As with many other New Games components, equipment is only a small part of the game. Don't let it become the game itself.

Your single most useful item of equipment will probably be a soft foam ball. We refer to them as Nerf balls in this book—the word Nerf is a trademark, but any brand will do.

In fact, you might want to experiment with brands, because the properties of foam balls differ from manufacturer to manufacturer. For instance, some foam balls are firm enough to bounce—a nice quality that can speed the pace of a game. The larger a ball, the more easily it can be seen and caught. Brightly colored balls add excitement to a game. In addition to the games that require an object to throw, you can use balls in games such as Loose Caboose and Clam Free to designate the person who is It.

Frisbees are manufactured by the Wham-O Company; other companies make flying discs of various sorts. Frisbees are great toys to toss around before a play session or use in a game, but make sure that all the players have Frisbee-tossing experience before you start a game like Frisbee Fakeout. Frisbees also make good markers for boundaries. Some companies manufacture soft foam flying discs that can be used in dodge-ball type games, and one company manufactures a disc made of nylon material, weighted at the edge, that you can fold and put in your pocket, handy for a sudden game of whatever, whenever.

Boffers (another trademark) are polyethylene swords. Their key quality is that you can swat someone with a Boffer and not hurt him (protective eye goggles are recommended). You can easily improvise your own swatter by rolling up a newspaper. Hardware stores carry three-foot sections of foam insulation for pipes that also works well. Boffer substitutes should be soft and flexible, without any sharp edges. Let all the players have a chance to hit and be hit by the swatter before the game starts, and make it clear that the desired swat is a noisy, painless "thwak" below the waist.

Earthball is the New Games Foundation's brand name for the six-foot canvas pushballs we sell. The Earthball has a replaceable vinyl bladder inside a canvas cover silk-screened with the outline of the continents. Each Earthball we sell comes with paints, for a do-it-yourself planet-painting party, and a vinyl-repair kit. You certainly don't need an Earthball to play New Games; but one never fails to draw a crowd. If you are lucky enough to have one handy, be sure you take the safety precautions outlined on pages 35 and 36 before you

start playing Space Chase or any other Earthball game.

A parachute is one piece of equipment that can add to the cohesiveness of a play session. It is especially useful with disabled players, because it allows them to participate in moving the chute according to their particular abilities. Look for them at surplus stores. The New Games Foundation sells "playchutes" made of ripstop synthetic fabric specifically for recreational purposes. If you have a parachute, you can spread it on the ground to form a play area or tie it between some trees to shelter a game of Rain. It's another nearly irresistible piece of play equipment. (More information about playchutes, Earthballs and Boffers, as well as reviews of other play equipment, can be found in the New Games Resource Catalog.)

The key to using equipment in New Games is improvisation and inspiration. Almost any item can be incorporated into a game (as long as it's safe) and could turn it into a brand new New Game. Balloons, Hula-Hoops, nylon tubular ropes, and balls of every composition and dimension have unlimited play potential. Just don't lose sight of the great games that require only smiles.

Specializing Play. In New Games, every group you play with is special. Your players, whoever they are, are unique. The only "right" way to play with them is to apply the New Games attitude and to let their preferences and needs shape the play session. But sometimes, knowing that isn't quite enough. Here are a few additional insights that may help you play with particular groups.

If you're playing with children, you probably won't have much difficulty generating lots of energy. You might, however, find it difficult to foster sharing and community awareness. Young children tend to be self-involved in their play. They'll consider it very important to be It and forget to use the link-up feature of Elbow Tag. They'll forget to pass the ball in Monarch. It may be difficult for them to maintain the group focus necessary for a game like Willow in the Wind.

To establish a more democratic play community among children, take advantage of the many trusting elements of New Games. Explain the rules clearly and stress the importance of strategy and teamwork. While the game is in progress, have the players raise their hands to indicate who hasn't been chosen or tagged, or who hasn't received the ball. The result might be a play session that takes both the children and you closer to the goal of empowered and trusting play.

If you're playing with a mixed group of children and adults, choose games carefully, or modify games, to make sure that the size discrepancies among the players don't create safety problems. Using two children to equal one adult in playing Yurt Circle is an example. Tap into the children's boundless energy and their natural capacity for fantasy to inspire the adults; use the adults to help guide the children toward awareness and responsibility.

As children get older, whether from age or experience, you may find that they're suspicious of games that are strange to them or that require them to risk being silly among their peers. You may have to warm up a group of inner-city kids or suburban junior-high schoolers with some familiar, goal-oriented games such as tag, and then gradually integrate elements

of ritual, fantasy, chanting, and humor into the play session. Once you've established their participation and trust, you can move on to more unusual or risky games.

New Games can provide an excellent opportunity for seniors to interact playfully. You might have to reduce the physical challenges in some games, but let the group, not your fears, guide you. The goal is,

as always, to provide safe fun. Active games such as Quick Line-up or Elbow Tag may be inappropriate for seniors, but most likely, if you slow them down dramatically or greatly shrink their boundaries, you can successfully adapt such games to their physical needs.

One hidden resource with seniors is fantasy. Although the elderly are often stereotyped as less playful, it might be simply that they've been

denied opportunities to play. Employing imagery, chanting, singing, and play-acting can add energy, creativity, and involvement to your play session, which will more than compensate for physical limitations.

New Games have been played successfully with a wide range of people who have physical or mental disabilities. The key to playing with such populations is to focus on what the players can do, rather than on what they can't do. For example, don't start out by trying to think of games that people confined to wheelchairs can play. Think of games that can be played by people who can throw balls, clap, sing, or guess. Think of the possibilities for pairing players with different abilities. And whatever game you suggest, make it a game that you think is fun and that you like to play. Your enthusiasm for the games will encourage the other players to get involved, and that will be more important than whether a particular game is "ideally" suited for a particular player.

Most important, when playing with any special population (and that includes everybody), keep your expectations open. Not everyone can play every game. But everyone can have the chance to play and to choose activities that they can enjoy. New Games provide a way to bring people of different abilities together. They can also give people with special needs a chance to exercise power and self-expression in a way not often realized in their everyday lives.

Adapting. By now, you've heard many times that in New Games you can change the rules. And indeed, there's nothing sacred about the form or structure of a New Game. We suggest you change games for the fun of it, but mostly we suggest you change games to adapt them to the specific needs of your play group.

Adapting games successfully depends on your powers of observation. It's up to you to watch and see what isn't working in a game or how it can be made more fun. Is the target so elusive in Triangle Tag that the chaser would rather play another game? Are the same players getting captured over and over in Giants/Elves/Wizards? Are the Jedi knights in Star Wars frozen before the game has really begun?

Most of the things you'll notice going awry in your games will be caused by an imbalance in the challenges they offer. Solving such a problem usually means tempering a challenge. Take a game like Broken Spoke. If some players are much faster runners than others, the slow runners will be frustrated and the fast runners will be bored. Change the locomotion so that everyone has to proceed by placing one foot directly in front of the other, heel to toe. With the speed of the game decreased, players of a

much wider range of locomoting ability can enjoy it.

You can also temper a game's challenge by reducing its dimensions. Shrinking the boundaries will tend to slow players—Octopus is an example. Making the playing area smaller will also make it easier to achieve the object of the game. If everyone stands in a smaller circle, it's easier to catch people with the Boffer in Swat and easier to catch the balls in Group Juggling. In both cases, making the game smaller will let you involve a broader range of abilities.

A third way of tempering the challenge is to alter the object of the game or the limitations imposed on achieving the object. For example, in Triangle Tag, if you let the chaser tag the target from across the triangle, the object of the game, tagging the target, becomes easier. Make the players in the triangle keep their hands on each other's shoulders and it becomes easier still. Both variations will let you successfully broaden the range of abilities in the game.

Without getting too involved in games theory, you can see that the speed of a game, its dimensions, and the ease of achieving its object are frequently interrelated. When you make a game slower, smaller, or easier, you'll generally be able to adapt it to a more diverse group.

Another way of broadening the appeal of a game is to turn individual challenges into shared challenges. If you play *How Do You Do?* in pairs you establish a common denominator among the players' abilities. The more that teamwork becomes a feature of games like *Clam Free* or *Star Wars*, the less likely the game is to become frustrating or boring for certain players. You can also broaden challenges by decentralizing the action. Add more balls or make more players *It*. The more kinds of activity there are going on at the same time, the more opportunities there are for people to find their own challenge level.

Keep in mind that you don't have to make each game slower or smaller or more diffused. Sometimes a game might not be working because it's not challenging enough. If the abilities of everyone in the group are evenly matched, go ahead and raise the challenge level.

Remember, too, that there's more to New Games than just physical challenge. Look for ways to increase the trust in a game or make it safer. Make the fantasy and the imagery more accessible by changing it to make it more relevant to your players. And however you adapt a game, let the players be involved in the process. When you do that, you'll come up with a game that responds to all of their abilities.

Inventing. *In one sense, you'll be inventing games whenever you play New Games, as you personalize and adapt each game to your group or follow suggestions for variations as they come up. Sometimes, however, we get together just for the purpose of creating a new New Game. We call this playing with games.*

To invent a new game, start by considering the elements common to every game. The most basic of these is the setting in which the game is to be played. It includes the physical environment—a grassy field, a gymnasium, a meeting room, a snowy hillside, a swimming pool—as well as the number and characteristics of the players. For example, you might want to invent a game that can be played by six teenagers at the beach, or by two dozen teachers attending a conference. You don't have to start with an imaginary setting, however. You can simply decide to invent a game on the spot for the people participating in your session, wherever you happen to be.

The object of the game is another element to consider. You might try to arrive at a victor through a process of elimination, as in Elephant/Palm Tree/Monkey. The point of Loose Caboose and Monarch is to capture the prey with a tag. In Frisbee Fakeout, the laurels will go to the best catchers, throwers, and strategists. Broken Spoke is basically a race, and the object of the game of Killer is to guess whodunit. Many New Games have combined objectives —in Lemonade the point is to solve the mime and capture players.

Another game element is structure. This includes the setting of boundaries, the organization of the players—in teams or in a formation or both—and the relationships between individual players. Often, the formation of players will determine the boundaries of the game, as in How Do You Do? And an example of player-to-player structure is the linkage feature of Elbow Tag.

Another element is the permitted action in the game. This includes the method of locomotion (running, crab-position crawling, remaining stationary), body movement (clapping, pointing, throwing, acting),

and methods of or limitations on communication (signaling, making noises, keeping eyes closed).

A game may also have more or less defined roles for the players. In simple tag, there are only two roles: You're either It or you're not. Elbow Tag involves three roles: the chaser, the runner, and the safe, linked players. Star Wars has specialized roles for the Jedi knights, as well as the frozen/ unfrozen roles for the rest of the players. In Knock Your Socks Off, everyone is simply a player until eliminated. In Zen Clap, eliminated players become hecklers. Frequently, a form of game action will be involved in switching players from one role to another.

The use of equipment can affect the physical structure of a game, its action, or its roles. Monarch is really a tag game, with the thrown ball becoming an extension of the players tagging ability. The character of a game that makes use of equipment is often determined by the properties of the item used. Imagine playing Frisbee Fakeout indoors with ping-pong balls.

A very important games component is ritual and fantasy. To fully appreciate this, you might try playing a game such as Samurai Warrior, Snowblind, or Killer stripped entirely of its imagery and play-acting elements, or Get Down or Lemonade without the chanting. If you can figure out a way to play them at all, you'll probably discover that they're not very engaging games without their creative-play components.

Very often, the fantasy of a game will suggest a form of game action. An example is Clam Free. That game provides for the player who is It to assume the fantasy role of a nuclear reactor. Taking that imagery further, the reactor-shutdown feature of the game evolved. The mere substitution of a fantasy can change the nature of a game, as when mythical creatures were added to Rock/Paper/Scissors from The New Games Book, resulting in Giants/Elves/Wizards.

There are several ways to proceed in inventing New Games. One is through adaptation. The process of adding, subtracting, or changing one component of a game at a time often results in a truly new New Game. A series of adaptations transformed Slaughter into Annihilation and then into Knock Your Socks Off. And Data Processing can provide new challenges and interactions if you add a limitation component—ask people to sort themselves, by birthday, let's say, without talking, using only sign language.

You might also see what happens when you combine two games. Some combinations to play with: How Do You Do? and Octopus, Zen Clap and Pile Up, This Is My Nose and Shoe Factory.

Another games-invention technique is to think of some game element that seems unique and build a

	Environment	Objective	Structure	Action	Roles	Equipment	Fantasy/Ritual
1	living room	achievement	circle	sitting	It/not It	balls	food
2	classroom	tagging	square	running	two teams	discs	mythology
3	auditorium	racing	opposing lines	jumping	three teams	ropes	movies/TV
4	gym	throwing	chain	crawling	partners	swatters	nature
5	field	capturing	bounded field	carrying	group	balloons	science fiction
6	beach	eliminating	combat zone	repelling	leaders	clothing	technology
7	woods	responding	safety zone	pulling	liberators	coins	song
8	snow/ice	guessing	pile	signaling	decoys	noisemakers	dance
9	water	scoring goals	back to back	eyes closed	impostors	boxes	chanting
0	outer space	participation	free form	no action	goalies	no equipment	counting

game around it. Knight's Move was created this way. We started with the three-step move of the knight in chess, and we quickly added a chessboard structure and two teams, white and black. We decided that whites had to face one direction and blacks the other purely as a practical way of identifying who was on which team. The chant, "Knight's move, check," helped us keep some order in the game and added some noisy reinforcement to the fantasy. As we played this game we discovered that the boundaries had to be based on the number of players. As a later refinement, we limited the tagging action by restricting players to tagging only with their shoulders, no lunges allowed. This permitted us to play the game with a large number of people while confined to a small, indoor setting such as a classroom.

A fourth approach to games inventing is to make an invent-a-game grid like the one pictured on this page, with ten ideas for each of the seven games components. (You'll have even more fun if you fill in your own rather than using ours.) Then choose a phone number, and come up with a combination of components. For example, 668-6901 would give you a game to be played on the beach that involved eliminating players from a pile by having them repel each other, making use of some players (or one player) as impostors. No equipment would be needed, and the game would have a food-inspired fantasy. Can you visualize the game if we call it Rotten Apple? Be prepared to improvise as your invention takes shape.

Inventing games is very much a trial-and-error proposition, and it requires an agreement among the players to enjoy experimenting with games and not worry about being entertained by the games themselves. The rewards are great, however, both in terms of furthering your understanding of games and in coming up with some exciting games in the process. Once you've made the playing of New Games a game in itself, you'll be ready to find others and say, "Tag, you're It!" and keep the New Games game going. ■

Games for Two Dozen

HIGH ACTIVITY
Broken Spoke
Loose Caboose
Wink
Clam Free
Monarch
Knock Your Socks Off
Elbow Tag

MEDIUM ACTIVITY
Yurt Circle
Body Snatchers
Lemonade
Jamaquack
Quick Lineup
Body Surfing
Cookie Machine

LOW ACTIVITY
Knight's Move
Data Processing
Human Compressor
Shoe Factory
Tableaux
Elephant/Palm Tree/Monkey
Rain

Broken Spoke

This game is played in many lands under many different names, but whatever it's called, it never fails to keep us on our toes.

We arrange ourselves like the spokes of a wheel, sitting cross-legged one behind the other in four or five lines of five or six people each. All of us in each of the spokes face the center, or hub, of the wheel.

One player starts the game as the caller. She walks around the outside of the wheel and breaks a spoke by tapping the last person in one of the lines. As she does so, she says either, "Come with me!" or "Go away!" The action that ensues depends on which command she spoke (we

couldn't resist!). The caller and everyone in the broken spoke race around the wheel and try to get back into line. If the caller said, "Come with me," the players run around the wheel in the same direction as the caller. If she said, "Go away," they run around in the opposite direction. (The caller always gets the inside track.) The last person to get back into line is the caller for the next round.

There's a lot of scrambling in this game, and all the people in the unbroken spokes are sitting ducks for a collision. Let's be sure that we play with a heightened safety awareness. We want only broken spokes—not broken folks. ■

Loose Caboose

Take the basic idea of a game like Elbow Tag, add a fantasy, and we can create a New Game with rather different qualities—such as this combination of tag and a railroad switchyard gone haywire.

To start, we set boundaries and form trains—each with a locomotive and three or four cars and each made up of players with their hands on the hips of the players in front of them. The number of trains depends on the number of players, but there should be at least three trains, and we need two additional people as well—one to be the switcher and the other to be (you guessed it!) the loose caboose.

The object of the game is for the switcher, who is armed with a Nerf ball, to try to tag the loose

caboose with the ball before the caboose can hook on to the back of a train. If the caboose does manage to link up, the locomotive of her train breaks away to become the new loose caboose.

If the switcher tags the caboose, the caboose becomes the new switcher, and the old switcher gets a free trip around the switchyard to hook on to the back of any train and release a locomotive as the new loose caboose.

The key feature of this game is that each train should do its utmost to avoid the loose caboose. This should make for more tagged cabooses, and thus keep the game moving at a fast pace.

For a variation, how about letting the switcher hook up to the end of a train, too, releasing a locomotive as a new switcher? The roles might get confusing in this version of the game, so each new switcher should announce his status by giving us a loud blast of his human steam whistle.

All aboard! ■

Wink

The name of this game suggests a subtle gesture, but subtlety is merely the prelude to one of our most spirited softwar games. Wink's combination of quick reflexes, physical action, and fast-paced role switching has made it one of our favorites when we want the chance to play hard.

We need an odd number of players. We pair off, and one member of each pair kneels or sits cross-legged in a circle, facing the center. The other member of each pair takes a kneeling position behind his partner, forming another circle just outside the first. Finally, the extra person, who becomes the first winker, joins the players who make up the outer circle, and a Frisbee or other object is used to mark the vacant place in front of her.

The action starts when the winker gives a wink to one of the people in the inner circle. This is the signal for the person winked at—the winkee—to try to tag the Frisbee while his partner tries to restrain him. The winkee has to escape his partner and get to the Frisbee before the rest of us can count to six. None of the players can stand up, and no one can move until after the wink.

The postwink scramble gets sorted out as follows: If the winkee gets to the Frisbee in time, he and

the winker form a new pair—the winkee behind the winker. The winkee's unsuccessful partner becomes the new winker. If, on the other hand, the winkee is restrained for the full count, he and his partner change places and the winker starts another round.

Wink can be a rough game, so some safety considerations are important. Of course, we need to make sure we're playing on a safe surface and that we're not wearing sharp jewelry or buckles. We must also keep in mind that we should use force only to match the force offered by our partners, and not simply prove we can overpower them. We want to enjoy playing hard without being afraid of getting hurt. And, of course, we need to make it comfortable for people to leave the game if they feel it's too rough for them.

Wink players will display surprising tenacity, but this is not just a battle of brawn. Brute strength can usually be outmaneuvered by a quick eye and slippery tactics. And here's a warning: Loose trousers are not recommended apparel for this game. The ultimate indignity in Wink is to get "pantsed." ∎

Clam Free

Whenever people come together in common cause, there's a perfect opportunity to strengthen the community through play. This New Game arose out of the Clamshell Alliance rally and alternative-energy fair in Seabrook, New Hampshire. Clam Free not only helped the participants focus on the purpose of the event, it turned out to be a terrific game in its own right and one that has become a favorite from Old Orchard Beach to Malibu.

We start by defining the boundaries of the playing field. One person volunteers to be the nuclear reactor and activates himself with a Frisbee or Nerf ball, preferably Day-Glo. The rest of us are clams, and we can so signify by being as happy as possible.

The object of the game is for the nuclear reactor to contaminate all the clams by tagging them with the Day-Glo device. Once contaminated, the clams become frozen in place.

As the reactor chases and tags the clams, it would appear that doomsday is just around the corner—at least for the hapless clams who are getting zapped one after another. There is hope, however. A frozen clam can be defrosted if two mobile clams manage to link elbows around her in a clamshell-like alliance and shout, "Clam free!"

Better yet, any clam that has been defrosted can join hands with other freed clams and these hand-holding clams are then immune from further radiation attacks by the reactor. And even better yet, if four or more hand-holding, immune clams

manage to encircle the reactor and shout, "Clam free!" the reactor must shut down for good.

We might want to adjust the rules (or even the fantasy) to make the game playable for different groups. And if the reactor seems to be getting the upper hand, we can always recruit more clams. ■

Monarch

There's no political theory intended in this game, but the fact remains that it starts with just a token monarchy amidst a sea of anarchy and ends with the monarchy ruling the entire territory. Though we won't get to witness the anarchist revolution in this game—we will see some lively dodge-ball-style action combined with close teamwork.

We set up the boundaries of the kingdom to accommodate the size of our playing group and choose one of us to be the monarch. She is armed with a Nerf ball as her only tangible symbol of royalty, and she has the power to convert others to the monarchy simply by hitting them with the ball.

The rest of us are the anarchists, and we are free to roam the kingdom at will. Our only aim is to escape being tapped by the royal Nerf. Once hit by the ball, an anarchist must announce his new status by raising his hand and shouting, "Monarch!"

These royal proclamations are not simply for show—they're a key to playing the game, for when a monarch has the ball, she's confined to her throne, so to speak, and can't move her feet. Her only choices are to try to hit one of the anarchists or to pass the ball to another monarch who might be in a better position to make a convert to royalty. By keeping the ball moving (and, as in all dodge-ball games, aimed safely below the waist), the monarchs should be able to increase their number and transform all the rabble into courtiers in due time.

If you're too much a proletarian or a populist at heart and can't get enthusiastic over the fantasy of this game, why not think of the monarchs as being of the orange-and-black butterfly variety? Their object? Trying to metamorphize a squirm-age of caterpillars. ■

Knock Your Socks Off

Here's a perfect example of how a game can evolve over time. This one actually started as Slaughter—a great softwar game that requires two teams on their knees, two medicine balls, two holes in soft ground, and offensive and defensive strategies (aimed at moving one team's ball into the other team's hole) that are just slightly less complicated than the Dallas Cowboys playbook. You can read all about it in *The New Games Book*.

Not too surprisingly, the National Slaughter League never made a go of it. Next came Annihilation, which is also included in *The New Games Book*. This game is much simpler: There are two teams, a defined soft playing area, and all the players have to stay on their hands and knees. There are no balls and no holes—the

object is for all the members of one team to push all the members of the other team off the playing area. Annihilation is still one of our favorite games when we want to play hard.

The persistent problem with the game, however, has been how to signify the two teams. We've never had enough advance notice to provide official Annihilation team uniforms, and the old standby, "Let's play shirts and skins!" is a wisecrack whose time has definitely passed. The best solution to the team-identification problem has been for one team to remove their hosiery and play All Sox vs. No Sox. Of course, in the process of annihilation, some of the All Sox have lost their stockings to their opponents, and from there

it has been but a stocking-footed hop to Knock Your Socks Off.

We begin this game with our socks on. A player is eliminated when both his socks have been removed by another player. We must keep within defined boundaries and stay on our knees. Socks should be pulled straight off our opponents' feet to avoid twisted appendages, and any player caught kicking another is subject to a one-sock-removal penalty (two socks and elimination, if the offense is flagrant). Eliminated players serve as referees.

Already, various versions of Knock Your Socks Off have evolved. The American Conference rules, for instance, specify team play, with the White and Grey Sox vs. the Colored Sox. The National Conference several years ago abandoned team play in favor of the free-for-all, and this form of the game is steadily gaining in popularity.

Serious note: We can have a lot of fun venting our aggressions in a softwar game like Knock Your Socks Off, but safety is always our first consideration. We must agree to use force only to match, not overpower, our opponents. This game should be played on a soft surface; players should remove their jewelry; and in a game that creates the sort of melee this one does, we should impose the Stop Rule—that is, when any player feels in physical danger, he should call, "Stop!" and the call should be repeated by the other players until the game comes to a halt.

Footnote: In the spring of 1981, the commissioner of the Universal Knock Your Socks Off League ruled that knee socks were illegal equipment (all socks must be pulled down to ankle length before play) and that any player caught wearing leotards would be fined for unsockspersonlike conduct. ■

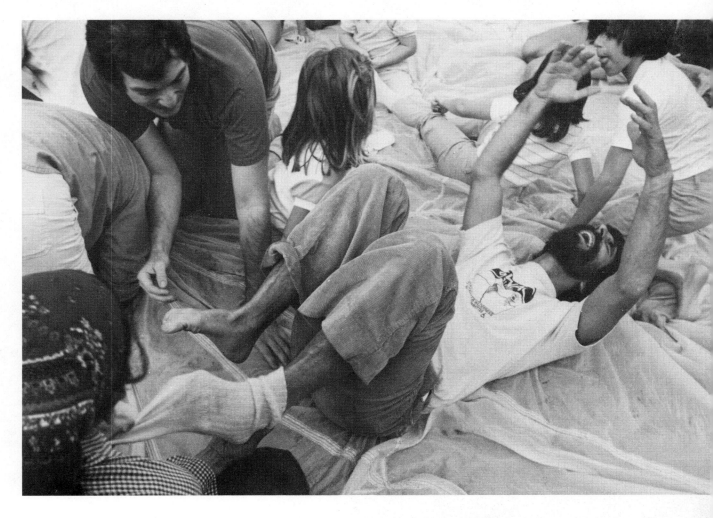

Elbow Tag

A simple twist on one of the world's oldest games transforms it into a new favorite, guaranteed to raise the activity level of virtually any group.

Let's divide into pairs and have each player link an elbow with his partner, keeping his outside elbow bent and his outside hand on his waist. We need one volunteer to be It and another to be the runner.

The person who is It tries to tag the runner, of course, but here's the twist: The runner can avoid being tagged by linking an elbow with the free elbow of any member of any pair on the playing field. When he does, he shouts, "Go!" and the other member of the pair must take off as the new runner, hotly pursued by the person who is It. If the runner is tagged, he's It, and his nemesis becomes the new runner.

All of us should act as referees to make sure that runners do take advantage of the link-up feature

of Elbow Tag. After all, we don't want to end up just watching Susie chase Tim around the block.

There is a lot of room for variation in this game. The pairs can be arranged in a circle or placed randomly around the field. Partners can face the same direction or opposite directions, in swing-your-partner style. The person who is It, as well as the runner, can be allowed to rest by linking an elbow with a pair and releasing a new player to be It.

However we play it, Elbow Tag should keep us all participating and panting no matter how old we are or what shape we're in. It's highly competitive and yet very forgiving, and it's a particularly good game for young children and adults to play together. ∎

Yurt Circle

The name of this game derives from that ingenious Mongolian nomads' tent in which the roof pushes against the walls in perfect equilibrium, keeping the structure standing. If we all work together, we can get our own yurt supporting itself in no time.

We form a circle with an even number of players. All of us face the center, standing almost shoulder to shoulder and holding hands. We then go around the circle and one person says, "In," the next says, "Out," and so on. When we're finished, each In should be standing between two Outs and vice versa.

Then we count to three, and the Ins lean toward the center of the circle while the Outs lean back. We all keep our feet stationary and support ourselves with our held hands. With a bit of practice, we can lean amazingly far forward and backward without falling.

Once our yurt is stable, we can try counting to three and having the Ins and the Outs switch roles while we continue holding hands. If we get really proficient, we can try switching back and forth in rhythm.

A yurt stays upright because each part is responsible for supporting the whole, with an interplay of forces in opposition and in harmony at the same time. What could be a better metaphor for New Games? ∎

Body Snatchers

This hybrid game came about at a New Games training sesssion in Virginia Beach, Virginia, when two games from *The New Games Book*, Vampire and Blob, were combined. It borrows its name from a classic sci-fi chiller, *Invasion of the Body Snatchers*, and like the movie, it is not for the faint of heart.

Body Snatchers begins with one player as the evil invader from outer space and the rest of us as normal, content average citizens. We mingle and go about our business the way average citizens do except for one thing—because we are blind to the impending threat from the body-snatching alien, we have to keep our eyes closed. (This game requires a referee to keep us average Joes and Janes from blindly wandering off.)

As a superior being, the invading body snatcher gets to keep his eyes open. He also gets to begin the earth's takeover by creeping up to an unsus-pecting citizen and pouncing on him, while making whatever bloodcurdling sound is in vogue among body snatchers these days. If the pounced-on citizen survives the leap in his blood pressure and heart rate, he becomes a body snatcher too. Now both body snatchers go off together in search of another victim and convert. As the body-snatching blob grows, we few surviving citizens, eyes still closed, can hear our numbers being reduced methodically and insidiously.

The final scene is, of course, too horrible to reveal, but the last survivor should receive a free pass to next Saturday's matinee or the next game. (Note: Theater doors *must* remain open during the entire performance of Body Snatchers to permit exit by any players who are not sci-fi/horror fans). ■

Lemonade

If we have a lemon, we can make lemonade, or just about anything we can imagine in this game that combines geographical adventures, inventive occupations, pantomime skills, quick reactions, and a dash for the finish line.

We divide into two teams, the actors and the guessers, and set up parallel goal lines about fifteen yards apart. Each team retires to its line. The actors go into a huddle and choose a geographical location and an occupation that is common there. They might consider Cape Cod fishermen or Texas cowboys or Hollywood film-makers, to name some *very* obvious examples. The guessers, in the meantime, are preparing themselves to figure out the geographical and occupational combination being concocted at the other end of the field.

Here's the way it's done. Each team lines up on its goal line and the actors start the ritual confrontation by taking two giant steps toward guesser territory, yelling, "Here we come!"

The guessers, matching advance with advance, also take two giant steps forward and yell back, "Where're you from?"

The actors step forward again and shout out the name of the geographical location they have chosen.

The guessers take two more giant steps and ask, "What's your trade?"

The actors reply, "Lemonade!" leaping forward again.

The guessers now take two final steps toward the actors with this challenge: "Well, show us some if you're not afraid!" If the choreography has worked, the two teams should now be lined up nose-to-nose in the center of the field.

The actors now get the chance to act out, in pantomime, their chosen occupation while the guessers try to guess it, shouting out possibilities at will and loud enough for everyone to hear. When a guesser figures out the mass mime and calls out the correct job, the actors must run back to their goal line before they are tagged by the guessers. Tagged actors join the guessing team, and the guessers become the actors for the next round.

Now, those actors in the photos have told us they're from the American River. What are they pantomiming? If we take a cue from our history books and the guy wearing the floppy hat, we can probably figure out their trade. ∎

Jamaquack

This wonderfully silly game was invented during a game-change session at a New Games Training in Springfield, Massachusetts, where it was discovered that to be a jamaquack is a never-to-be-forgotten experience.

Jamaquacks are rare birds from southern Australia. Being from down under, they always stand bent over, with their hands grasping their calves or ankles, and shuffle along backward. They are nocturnal by preference, and when they are out and about in daylight, they always keep their eyes closed. Day or night, they communicate with each other by quacking constantly, ceasing only to take a breath. (Jamaquacks must sometimes be reminded to take enough breaths to keep from becoming that other rare bird, the dizzy-crested blood rusher.)

Since jamaquacks are always trying to wander off somewhere, only a third of us can be jamaquacks at a time. The rest of us must form a jamaquack pen by holding hands in a circle, facing the center. Two of us create a hole in the pen by dropping our hands.

The jamaquacks gather in the middle of the pen, heads together, and begin quacking and moving backward with their eyes closed, trying to find the way out. While the foolish birds are engaged in their trial-and-error escape attempts, those of us forming the circle do our best to jam the quacks back inside the pen by gently knee-bumping them if they back into us.

Once outside the circle (their objective), the jamaquacks can finally stand upright and open their eyes, but they should keep quacking to let their species mates locate the hole.

Once you've seen a jamaquack, we're sure you'll want to be one. ∎

This is one of the few New Games that's played in a square rather than a circle. It also is a great way for four teams to test wits and group spirit.

We start by lining up shoulder to shoulder in four teams, each team forming one side of the square, with everyone facing the center. One person goes into the center of the square as the spinner. She stands still for a minute, facing one of the

teams, and this a really crucial moment in the game. Each team member has to remember, first, the order in which his team is lined up—that is, who he is next to in line—and second, where his team is lined up in relation to the spinner. A team can be facing the spinner; it can be to her left or right side; or it can be behind her. If we're not clear on this, we're going to be very lost, very soon.

Once we all know where we are, the spinner spins around and when she comes to a stop (facing a different team, presumably) she calls, "Quick lineup!" That's the signal for the teams to regroup around the spinner in their *original* positions; that is, to the spinner's front, left, right, or back. To do this everyone will have to scramble across or around the square (without collisions, please!) and get into the right spot in relation to the spinner and his teammates.

As soon as each team is back in its original order and its original orientation to the spinner, all its members join raised hands and shout, "Quick lineup!" indicating that their team is without question the most together of the four.

The spinner can continue to spin and stop as long as she wants, launching the teams on their dash to put matters back in order. Players should be warned of some typical spinner tricks: coming to a stop in the same position she was in in the last round or bending over. And what would we do if the spinner came to a stop lying on her stomach? ∎

Body Surfing

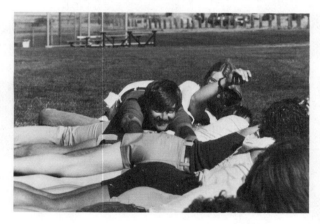

Even if we've never seen the ocean, we need not be denied the joys of being carried along on a rolling wave. We simply round up enough bodies to get the surf up and each of us can catch a gentle breaker for a ride.

First, let's remove sharp jewelry and belt buckles. Then we all lie face down side by side, spaced about a body's width apart to form a long human breaker. A player kneels at one end of the line of bodies and launches himself onto the surface, belly down with his arms outstretched.

Now it's time for some wave action. Those at the beginning of the line start rolling over continuously in the same direction. As the surfer moves onto new players, they roll as well. If we get the movement down just right, we will be able to propel the surfer safely forward on a rippling wave to the beach at the other end of the line. He then lies down and becomes part of the wave, and the person at the head of the line gets to try her surfing skills.

You'll notice that the wave will creep forward as the surfing action proceeds, so make sure that there's room for it to advance and that the area is safe for rolling bodies. If we're prepared to keep this game going long enough, we can start somewhere on the prairie and roll all the way to the beach. ■

Cookie Machine

Who wouldn't leap at the chance to become the cookie of his choice? Each player provides the ingredients, and we all supply the oven.

First, we should remove our watches or any jewelry on our hands. Then we form two lines that face each other, all of us standing shoulder to shoulder with our elbows bent and our forearms in front of us, palms up. Our forearms should alternate—one player's arms should each be flanked by the arms of players across from him. Everyone must bunch together very closely, with one foot forward and one foot back for balance. Now we've got a solidly built oven with a conveyor belt running down the middle.

Just before baking, each cookie should remove his glasses, if he wears them, and his belt buckle, if it is sharp. Then he stands at one end of the oven, announces what kind of cookie he wants to be, and slides himself into the oven. The rest of us are bakers and we chant his cookie choice ("Chocolate chip, chocolate chip") as we bounce him along the conveyor belt, turning him over halfway through, until he pops out the other end, freshly baked.

We can't afford any broken cookies in this bakery, so we must handle the dough with extreme care and have two strong bakers available to ease each cookie out of the oven. After they make sure the cookie is done (that is, not dizzy), the cookie joins the oven.

Everyone should get a chance to invent his own cookie. When we've all been baked to a golden brown, how about inventing a game called Milk and Cookies! ■

Knight's Move

We don't have to be whiz kids or human computers to play this New Games version of chess. We play with just one type of piece, and by the time the game has progressed to checkmate, everyone's a winner.

In our version, we're all knights and our basic move is just like that of the chessboard piece. We can take one step forward or back and two steps to the right or left, or we can take two steps forward or back and one step to the right or left. So there are eight three-step patterns we can follow.

Once we've all got the moves perfected, we can play the game. We set up boundaries so that we have a rectangular playing field, basing the size of the field on the number of players. One or two of us start at one end of the field as the black knights, and the rest of us line up at the other end as the white knights.

We begin a three-count chant: "Knight's move, check!" At each count, we take a step according

to one of the knight's-move patterns. At the end of the chant, everyone pauses for a moment and the black knights reach out and try to tag as many players as possible—at this point, no players, black or white, can move their feet. Tagged white knights turn around and face the same direction as the black players—and they too become taggers. Black-knight taggers always face one direction, and the untagged white knights always face the other direction.

Round by round, more players will join the taggers, and the final moves will involve a single untagged player being trapped by everyone else three-stepping in to tag him.

Once we're Knight's Move masters, how about adding a few rooks and bishops? ∎

	3	2	3	
3	2	1	2	3
		START		
3	2	1	2	3
	3	2	3	

Data Processing

It's always fun to find out exactly who we're playing with. Here are some ways to sort through a lot of information without using a single silicon chip.

How about arranging ourselves in a line according to height? Let's all mingle, and those who are shorter head for the front of the line; those who are taller go to the back. We can see how long it takes us to put everyone in order. P.S. We keep our eyes closed.

We can also arrange ourselves by first names, in alphabetical order. If we shake hands as we sort things out, we can get to know each other in the process. Or we can sort the states or countries in which we were born, or maybe our favorite ice cream flavors. What other data would we like to know about our group?

How about sorting birthdays in chronological order. Believe it or not, if we've got two dozen people, there's a better than fifty-fifty chance that two of us will share a birthday. (For math enthusiasts, the proof is in figuring the probability of there being *no* common birthdays. The chances of two people not having the same birthday are 364 in 365—not counting Leap Year Day. Add a third person, and the chances are the probability of the first two not sharing a birthday *times* the probability of the third person having still a different birthday. With four people, the probability becomes $364/365 \times 363/365 \times 362/365 = .9836439$; in other words, there's about a ninety-eight percent chance that four people will *not* share a birthday. Get out your calculator and keep going and you'll see that by the time you get to twenty-three people, the chances of no shared birthdays have dropped to 49.27019 percent. Oops! We did promise no silicon chips.)

When we're all lined up by birthdays, we can shout them out in order, from New Year's Day to New Year's Eve. How about some group cheers for each of the zodiac signs? Now we're all ready to invent a game for twelve teams. ■

Human Compressor

This is a balloon game that doesn't require us to buy any balloons, because all the balloons we need—every size, shape, and color—are always at hand, just waiting to be inflated. This is a great way to get warmed up by stretching our bodies and our imaginations.

The first thing we need is a volunteer to be the compressor. The rest of us lie flat on the ground, as limp as, well, uninflated balloons.

The compressor starts to huff and puff and do deep knee bends, or whatever exactly compressors do, while we balloons start to inflate. As the compressor fills us with air, we puff out our cheeks, stretch out our arms, and assume whatever balloon shapes we can imagine. Then the compressor can tie us off and set us free to float in the breeze, bump into each other, and generally do balloony things. (The Macy's Thanksgiving Day Parade could be an inspiration.)

There are several ways to end this game. The compressor can produce a long, sharp pin (imaginary, of course) and pop us one by one, or we can let all our air out at the same time and spin, snap, and shoot around in balloonlike random motion, keeping in mind that real deflated balloons aren't afraid of flopping down one on top of the other. One more reminder—balloons make noise when they lose their air, and Human Compressor is a natural for displaying our most creative, and perhaps otherwise socially unacceptable, mouth sounds. ∎

Shoe Factory

This game is an amazing feat (pun definitely intended). It demonstrates that, no matter how much chaos we create, there's always a way to put matters back in order. It also makes use of one of the most neglected pieces of play equipment in our closets—the common shoe.

We start by standing in a circle, and with the high ritual that this game deserves, we remove our

shoes and place them in a ceremonial pile in the center. Next, we all take three giant steps toward the pile, and everyone selects an unmatched pair of shoes, neither of which are his own.

Now we have two options. One is to close our eyes and try to identify the owners of the shoes we've selected. (The name of this game is actually Olfactory.) Most people, however, upon being given this option, choose the second, which requires each player to put on the shoes he has selected. If he has selected a sleek new High Techno brand running shoe, size 6A, and he is blessed with size 13EEE feet, he should just slip his toes in the shoe so he doesn't turn it into a Low Trashmo.

Once we're all standing around wearing two strange shoes, the peak pedal experience begins. As we all chant, "Shoe! Shoe! Shoe!" we shuffle around and try to find the people who are wearing the mates to our shoes. When we do find them, we keep the matching feet together so that all the shoes are in proper pairs. This process will probably result in a tangled living sculpture that's a veritable orthopedic Gordian knot, but ideally, we should find ourselves in some semblance of a circle.

"But where are *my* shoes?" We can answer that question with a single elegant move. We simply slip out of our captive footwear, leaving two dozen neatly arranged pairs of shoes waiting to be reclaimed by their rightful and grateful owners. ■

Tableaux

Here's an opportunity to prove that we can be anything we want to be.

We form two groups with six to twelve players in each group. One group chooses a scene or an event that they would like to see re-created. They might suggest, for example, a tableau representing dental hygiene. It's then up to the other group

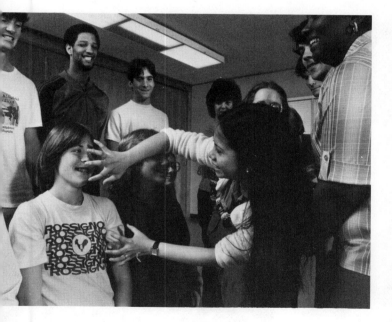

to put on their most inspired performance of "Dental Hygiene" using individuals to represent different objects or parts of the action.

What goes into the making of a Tableaux tour de force? The scenes or events with the most creative potential will have many specific elements that can be performed. It's really up to the nonperforming team to come up with imaginative suggestions for the tableaux.

The performing team takes a few minutes to decide on individual roles. They should think of ways that one person, or several people combined, can represent elements of the scene or suggest action. Then the performance begins!

In "Dental Hygiene," for example, we can have players represent molars, bicuspids, and incisors; we can create a human toothpaste tube with a cap and human toothpaste oozing out of it; we can select someone to be a bristly toothbrush; and we can finish the routine with some anthropomorphized dental floss. If we're really prepared to go all out for an unforgettable performance, how about a group gargle?

Of course, the best tableaux are the ones we think up ourselves, but in case we're stuck for starters, we can try "Bowling Alley" (with automatic pinspotters); "Bacon, Egg, and Waffle Breakfast" (with freshly squeezed orange juice); "Gas Station" (with a free car wash with fill-up); or "Supermarket Checkout" (with all produce weighed and bagged).

Get the picture? ■

Elephant/Palm Tree/Monkey

The cast of jungle characters in this game shifts so quickly that it's hard to keep track of who or what we're supposed to be. Don't worry—the real fun is in leaving our everyday world for faraway play places.

Our jungle world is made up of elephants, palm trees, and monkeys, each represented by a three-person pose. An elephant is composed of one person who turns himself into a long trunk and two other players, one on each side, who become large floppy ears. A palm tree has a tall trunk that reaches for the sky, flanked by two arching branches. Monkeys always travel in threes, and when confronted, they assume the classic "Hear no evil, see no evil, speak no evil" pose.

Before we begin to play, we should form a circle and practice making the three characters. Players should learn all three roles that go into each character's pose.

The game begins when one player steps into the center of the circle to be the spinner. He twirls around with his finger pointed while the rest of us set the mood by making jungle sounds.

The spinner comes to a halt with his finger pointing at one of us, and he calls out the name of one of the characters. The person pointed to must assume the central part of that character's pose, and the players on either side must complete the picture. All three have to strike the pose before the rest of us can shout, "Elephant, palm tree, monkey!" Whoever gets most fouled up by making the wrong move or by making a late move, gets to be the spinner for the next round.

If jungles don't fascinate us, we can create other fantasy settings—a farm, a mountaintop, a city park—and populate them with any three characters made up of three posing players. We can make the game more challenging by adding characters, increasing the number of people required for each pose, or using more than one spinner in the center of the circle.

When we've become pros at this game, we should be in fine shape for a creative round of Tableaux. ∎

Rain

We wanted to play outside today, but the sky is heavy with low gray clouds, there's an incessant drizzle filtering onto every leaf and blade of grass, and the weatherperson warned us to expect felines and canines and perhaps taxicabs falling from the sky. No matter, we'll play Rain.

We sit in a circle, facing the center. We close our eyes, pausing for a moment or two of quiet while each of us gets ready to repeat the sound the person on his right will be making.

We all keep our eyes closed, and the rainstorm gets underway as the leader rubs his palms together, back and forth. The person to his left joins him, and then the person to her left, and then the next person, and so on around the circle until everyone is rubbing palms and we can listen to the drizzling rain building in intensity.

When the leader hears the drizzle sound being made by the person on his right, he starts snapping his fingers. One by one around the circle, we replace palm rubbing with finger snapping, and the sprinkling rain turns into a steady patter. When the snapping action has been picked up by everyone, the leader switches to hand clapping, and we all follow in turn. We're hearing a hard rain now.

Our storm builds into a downpour as the leader begins slapping his thighs. Then the skies open and thunder crashes as the next round has us stomping our feet.

And then the storm subsides, just as it grew—foot stomping, thigh slapping, hand clapping, finger snapping, and back to palm rubbing. (If we're having trouble hearing the changes, we can alert our neighbors with a gentle nudge each time we switch from one action to the next.)

For the last round, the leader stops rubbing his palms and takes the hand of the person on his left, as each of us does in turn around the circle until there's silence once again. When we open our eyes, perhaps the sun will have appeared. ∎

The Big Game

Perhaps by now you've learned some of the games in this book and played them with your friends, coworkers, or clients. Maybe you've changed some of the rules or made up some games of your own. You might have organized and led a New Games play session as part of your work or volunteer activities. Possibly you've seen that the New Games attitude toward play can be incorporated into a traditional recreation program with which you're involved. Or perhaps you've been intrigued by reading about New Games but still aren't sure how they can work for you.

Over the years, we've received thousands of letters from people who have used New Games in different situations, with different players, in different environments. What follows is a sampling of stories from people who have each taken New Games home in a different way.

As you'll see, it doesn't matter where you are or what game you play. What matters is that you believe in the value of play. Play is contagious. Start playing and others will join you.

"We were on a river trip with people from an outreach recreation program—two blind women, three men in wheelchairs, two people with speech difficulties due to cerebral palsy, and eight guides (me included) and aides. We pulled into an eddy and someone suggested that we play a game. Having been labeled as the games person, I was on the spot. What game could we play sitting in boats with such a diverse group? Movement was out of the question; so were games requiring sight. And I wanted a game that would have some relevancy to where we were and what we were doing.

"I asked everyone to choose a word that described how they were feeling at that moment. 'Excited,' 'Adventuresome,' 'Cold,' 'Tired,' 'Exhilarated,' came the replies. After we all learned each other's words, I began by saying someone's word; then the person whose word I said had to follow with someone else's word. Those of us who could, set up a rhythm by tapping the side of the boat. We played a few rounds. Amazingly, the people with the greatest speech difficulties chose the hardest words and were the quickest to respond. There was much laughter.

"For the next three days, we fifteen people shared a secret identity.

Whenever someone spoke one of the words in normal conversation, the person whose word it was would immediately respond with another of the words. It helped us to be playful throughout the trip; it brought us together with a shared vocabulary."

■

"I was at a friend's birthday party and realized that everyone was spread throughout the living room, dining room, and kitchen. People were relating in small groups, but there wasn't any large group interaction and, most importantly, there wasn't any focus on the birthday person. I thought, Time for a game. But what game? And was I willing to take the big risk and get these people playing?

"I decided to go for it and try Get Down. Would everyone join in? Fortunately, I knew I could count on the birthday person to help get things started. People picked up on the game slowly at first; but once everyone was into the rhythm, I began to wonder if the game would ever end. We chanted at the tops of our lungs, then very softly, then in funny voices. We were having a great time.

"When that game finally wound down, we wanted to keep on playing. We tried Data Processing. We played Behavior Modification in teams, the most intensely competitive game of Zen Clap I've ever witnessed, and a game of Killer in which the sneaky killer got every last one of us. Then people started suggesting more games they remembered: Thumper and Who Started the Motion. It was after 2 a.m. when Rain brought the games to a close. It had all started with a very risky Get Down."

■

"We were backpacking along a beach and reached a tide-pool area. We started playing Bola with a long kelp root. That turned into an impromptu game of Catch the Kelp Dragon's Tail. We began to create our own fantasy kingdom, decorating ourselves with seaweed and driftwood. We became kings of the Crustacea and queens of the Anemone. In pantomine, we fantasized jumping off the high cliffs into the sea. A few years ago, I would have jumped off a real cliff just for the thrill, but the thought of doing mime would have sent me into waves of fear. The fantasy leaps we took that day covered more distance than any earthly leaps could."

■

"We were scheduled to make a New Games presentation as part of a teachers convention, and found ourselves in a small theater with a stage and rows of seats bolted to the floor. The stage was too small to play most active games, and at first we doubted that we'd be able to play at all. All of the lights in the theater could be dimmed, however, so we decided to take advantage of our unique play space by playing Sardines. With the lights out, one player hid. As each of the other players found the hidden player, they hid along with him. There aren't many places to hide forty people in a theater, so the real challenge was to keep all the sardines from giggling and whispering and making themselves even easier to locate. When everyone had finally stumbled on the hiding place—among the seats in the middle of the theater—the lights were turned on to reveal a mass of bodies on, under, and in between the rows of seats.

"From there, we played other creative-play games like Body Snatchers, Samurai Warrior, Shoe Factory, Mime Rhyme, and Tableaux. The teachers were transformed into a noisy, giggling group of active players. We were enjoying the games so much that people from other meetings interrupted several times to ask us to be quiet because other groups, hearing our laughter, wanted to come join us."

■

"We had been asked to come to a company picnic. It seemed like a perfect occasion to play. But everyone was unsure of how the company hierarchy should be carried over to the picnic. All people were doing was eating a lot—safe behavior. We knew a game with somewhat bizarre behavior, like Tableaux, might not go over at first. What could we play that would be more familiar? We decided to try Ultimate Nerf, which is similar to a lot of field games and might be easier for people to play.

"We rounded up a few people, luring them solely with the prospect of playing a game called Ultimate Nerf. We were careful not to make it sound too much like football so no one would be influenced by prior experiences. Suddenly, instead of eating and talking, people were running and jumping and catching and throwing. Work relationship patterns were forgotten as the teams formed patterns on the field trying to snatch the ball. It's hard to remain formal with someone when you're both chasing after a Day-Glo foam ball."

■

"We were conducting a New Games Festival at a correctional residential camp for adolescent boys. The boys were suspicious at first, and we felt uneasy, too, being locked in and under the watchful eyes of guards. Then someone started a game of Wink. It was an instant hit—the perfect occasion for a soft-war game. We all joined in and played very hard, but no one lost sight of the fact that we were playing. We were laughing and cheering and forgetting who was a resident and who was a New Games leader. What had started as a single game expanded to a three-ring Wink festival.

"All this activity was almost too much for the camp staff to bear. I was in the middle of one of the games and saw one of the staff standing to the side, watching. Some people tried to get him into the game. 'No, I'm the supervisor,' he said, crossing his arms across his chest. I looked up at him and said, 'No, I'm the supervisor now, and you can play.' Then I thought, Uh-oh, there he goes, walking away.

"I got someone to take my place and went over to him. We talked a bit. He said he had a bad knee and couldn't kneel, and furthermore, he was wearing his good pants and couldn't get them dirty. 'I have just the game for you then.' I taught him Quick Draw. He got into it and was pretty good. I taught him Me Switch. He was good at that too. We were laughing. He was having fun.

"We wandered back to the Wink game. The next time I saw him, he was kneeling behind his Wink partner, watching the winker intently, ready to make his move.
He played Wink the rest of the afternoon."

■

"I was in charge of a study hall in our library when there was a sudden power outage and the lights went out. After a few minutes of sitting in darkness with no prospect of the return of the lights, I asked a few students closest to me if they wanted to play a game. About six or eight of us gathered in a circle and we began a number game with rhythmic counting, a paying-attention game. Misses were punctuated and recorded by laughter. More players joined the game. When the lights finally came back on about thirty minutes later, they revealed four students from another room and one teacher who had wandered in from the hall to join us."

■

"We were making a plane connection in New Orleans International Airport. To get to the gates, we were traveling on a rolling concourse with dramatic spot-effect lighting. Suddenly the idea hit me. I asked my friend to hold my travel bag, and when we came to one of the circles of light, I did a little improvisational dance step. Then I nonchalantly took back my bag.

"'What do you think you're doing?' my friend asked. I told her it felt good and she ought to try it. At the next light, with a bit of encouragement from me, she did a little jig. At the next light, we performed a tango. The final light on the concourse showcased a spirited, if slightly inelegant, pas de deux.

"While we were waiting in line at the gate for our seat assignments, a rotund, middle-aged, cigar-puffing businessman, tie undone, tapped me on the shoulder. 'I saw what you did back there,' he said. Embarrassed, I admitted that we had gotten a little carried away. 'No,' he said, 'It was great! I've just had the worst business week of my life, and you just made my day.'

"My friend and I flashed a glance at each other. 'Not yet, we haven't!' We held his briefcase and escorted him to the nearest spotlight. He did a little twist. Our businessman was laughing. The whole line applauded."

■

"It's a matter of expectations. We were doing a play session at a state mental hospital. The referees were therapists, staff, and hospital volunteers. We were going to play for an hour or so with some of their clients. We thought we'd start with a game of Spirals—always a good place to begin. 'Everyone form a circle,' we said. But the clients weren't able to hold hands with each other. Some were in wheelchairs. Some were wandering off. Spirals seemed to be too complicated. We modified our suggestion: 'Let's just start walking.'

"With many false starts, we finally began walking in a circle. 'Who's got a song?' one of us asked. We began singing as we conducted a modified Follow the Leader. The clients didn't know where it was leading. We didn't either. We kept singing. Suddenly, it didn't matter where we were going. We loved moving around. We loved singing. We didn't want to stop.

"Was it a game? Well, maybe not. But it was play." ■

The More the Better

HIGH ACTIVITY

Octopus
Everybody's It
Space Chase
More Earthball Games

MEDIUM ACTIVITY

People to People
Giants/Elves/Wizards
Swamp Chute
More Parachute Games

LOW ACTIVITY

Vortex
Psychic Shake
Get Down

Octopus

We're told that octopusses (or is it *octopi*?) are not really as malevolent as most of us assume, despite the bad press caused by those awful sucker-covered tentacles. No matter, their perhaps undeserved reputation does lend a wonderfully dramatic and threatening fantasy to this game.

An octopus needs an ocean, of course, and we create one from a playing field with a goal at either end. Most of us are going to start this game as fishes, but one of us must volunteer to be the octopus, who is armed with a Nerf ball. The object of the game is for the octopus to eat the poor little fishes by tagging or hitting them with the ball; thereby growing his awful tentacles so he can eat more fishes.

The octopus roams the ocean while the rest of us fishes gather behind one of the goal lines. Then the octopus calls out, "Octopus, octopus, swim in my ocean!" At this command, the fishes must swim (run, walk, hop, or whatever we agree upon) across the ocean to the opposite goal. If one is tagged or hit by the ball, he is frozen in place, facing the direction in which he was swimming. All tagged fishes become octopus tentacles in the next round. And when the hungry octopus again invites the fishes to swim in his ocean, they can be tagged by the outstretched arms of the stationary tentacles, as well as by the roaming octopus.

After each round, as more fishes get devoured the octopus's tentacles multiply. When there are only a few fish survivors, we can prolong their lives a bit by having all the tentacles close their eyes, thus making it more difficult for them to snare their fish meal.

But the end is inevitable—one giant octopus filling the ocean with his slimy, sucker-covered, writhing tentacles. Yech! No wonder octopusses (*octopi*?) have got such a bad name. ∎

Everybody's It

This game provides a good introduction to a few variations on the time-honored game of tag. The next time we're in the mood to chase each other and say, "You're It," we can try these three tags and a tickle.

Let's start with the game of Everybody's It proper, which has been billed as the world's fastest game. There are two rules: (1) everybody is It, and (2) when a player is tagged, he's frozen. The game starts with each of us looking around and realizing that every other player is the enemy. Then, all together, we ask, "What's the name of this game?" When the answer comes, the game starts—and quickly ends.

Now that we've all been It, we can try Hospital Tag. The first time a player is tagged, he's got to keep one hand on the spot where he was tagged. The next time, he must keep his other hand on the second spot. Three tags and he's frozen. The last person frozen is It.

Or there's always Freezer-Defroster Tag. In this one, a tagged player must immediately freeze into a bent-over shape resembling a croquet hoop and stay that way until an untagged player manages to defrost him by crawling through the hoop.

When we get tired of playing tag, we can try Tickle a Pickle. First, everyone decides what kind of pickle he wants to be. Dill? Sweet? Gherkin? Kosher? Has everybody decided? Now, what's the name of this game? (This one is a good excuse to exercise our funny bones.) ∎

Space Chase

When people think of New Games, they often conjure up the image of the Earthball, that colossal sphere that is six feet in diameter and painted with the features of the whole earth. All over the world, we seem to be known as the folks with the big ball. We will never run out of Earthball games, and here's a new one that lets us have a ball playing with our planet as it races through space.

To get the game underway, we form two concentric circles—a large one composed of people standing about an arm's length apart facing inward, and a smaller circle, inside the large one, composed of people facing outward. This donut-shaped formation defines the earth's orbit.

Now we place the Earthball between the two circles and start it rolling around the orbit. With a little coordination and a lot of enthusiasm, we can soon send it smoothly speeding around the circle on its seasonal journey.

Then we get to play tag with the whole world—literally. When the Earthball is on the opposite side of the orbit, one of us steps into the pathway between the circles to become a cometlike racer through space. As we shoot the Earthball around its orbit, the racing space chaser tries to catch up with the earth and tag it.

But the space chaser should be forewarned: Those of us in the circles will be trying to accelerate the earth so that it catches up with the chaser from behind. It's an unforgettable experience to be eclipsed by an Earthball!

This orbital steeplechase is sometimes called Terra Tag. Let's make sure that we keep in mind the safety of the space chaser so that the game doesn't turn into Terror Tag.

More Earthball Games. If we've got an Earthball handy, we can play some of the other great Earthball games described in *The New Games Book*: Orbit, Planet Pass, Ball Crawl, and Chute Ball. In all games with the Earthball, however, we should be aware that it's a very special item of play equipment.

No one can really imagine what it's like to roll, bounce, or jump on a six-foot-high ball that often behaves as though it has a will of its own. It's bigger, heavier, and more erratic than you think. So before we play any Earthball games, we should make sure that every player has had a chance to get the feel of the ball.

If we have small children in our game, we should start out with Down Under, in which we kneel in a circle and see how fast we can pass the Earthball around. That ball looms a lot larger from a seven-year-old's perspective.

Let's get together in pairs and play Hemisphere Haunch, by batting the Earthball back and forth using our butts and hips. In Polar Route we join hands over the top of the Earthball and use it as a giant rocker. We'll soon discover than an Earthball is a lot bigger than both of us.

People always want to play King (or Queen) of theWorld on an Earthball. Because this round mass of rubber and canvas rolls *very* easily, there should always be three spotters close at hand whenever anyone attempts to kneel (no standing please!) at the North Pole.

Finally, here are some names for yet-to-be-invented Earthball games: Global Reach, Magellan, Prime Meridian, and As the World Turns. Get inspired, but remember: We should never turn an Earthball loose among inexperienced, unsupervised players. If we remember to show understanding and respect for this big ball we call the earth, we'll be able to create and share all our games in safety and with a truly playful spirit. ∎

People to People

Getting people together is the object of just about every New Game, and People to People explores just how many ways it can be done.

We pair up and stand in a circle, facing one player in the center, who is the leader. The leader sets a beat by clapping or snapping his fingers and chanting, "People to people." We're not going to let him do a solo, so we join in the chant too.

Once we're all caught up in the act, the leader substitutes the name of a body part for the word *people* in the chant, keeping the same rhythm, of course. "Back to back," he might say, and as we repeat the chant, we let our bodies follow the directions and assume, with our partners, what-

ever imaginative position the leader's chant has suggested. If he says, "Hip to hip," we bump hips; if he says, "Knee to knee," we face each other and touch knees. Matching body part to body part we continue until the leader shouts, "People to people!"

That's the signal for everyone to scamper about and find a new partner. The leader gets lost in the shuffle and finds a partner too. Unless an extra player sneaked in somewhere, there should be a new odd person out. She gets rewarded by becoming the new leader and continuing the chant, letting propriety be her only guide as to what body parts she directs us to connect next. (No X-rated instructions, please.)

A variation on this anatomical romp is Cumulative People to People, in which all the players are covered with imaginary glue and stick to each other wherever they are directed to touch. This version of the game will inevitably lead to a torturous tangle of human flypaper. By then, it's time for a new game. May we suggest Taffy Pull? ∎

Giants/Elves/ Wizards

Anyone who's played Rock/Paper/Scissors, which was described in *The New Games Book*, knows how wonderful that game is for getting everybody into the New Games act. Over the years, R/P/S has picked up a fantasy setting, new rituals, and a bit more body language, and it has emerged as this superb game for all of us creatures with imaginations.

We play this game in a kingdom inhabited by three very different types of beings: the giants, who stand on their toes, stretch their bodies as tall as possible, spread their arms, look very, very fierce, and shout, "Giants!" as loudly as they can; the elves, who squat down and pull in their shoulders and generally look very, very tiny as they barely peep their name; and the wizards, who stand hunched over with their hands thrust forward in the best spell-casting fashion intoning their name, "Wizzzzzards," in as weird and magical a manner as you can imagine.

The politics of this kingdom are such that no one of the three kinds of beings is absolutely more or less powerful than *all* the others. The giants are, of course, very strong and can easily overpower

the tiny elves; however, the giants are also rather stupid, and thus are easily fooled by the wizards' sorcery. And although the puny elves can be overcome by the giants, they are rather clever and can trick the wizards into casting the wrong spells. The wizards can fool the giants, but not the wily elves. So—giants beat elves, who beat wizards, who beat giants.

Once we've practiced each of the characters in our mythic drama and remembered their pecking order, we're ready to play the game. We form two teams, each with a goal line at either end of a field about fifteen yards long. Each team retires to its goal line, goes into a huddle, and decides which of the three charcters its members will portray.

The teams then face off in the center between the goals and start a four-part chant. On the first three counts, everyone says, "Giants, elves, wizards," assuming the proper voice and stance for each character. On the fourth and final count, each team shouts the name of its chosen character while taking the appropriate posture.

If we end up with elves facing giants, the giants can capture the elves by tagging them as they run for safety behind their own goal line. Or it could be elves chasing wizards or wizards chasing giants. Any player who is tagged by the overpowering team before reaching his goal line becomes part of that team. (To deal with the possibility of both teams choosing the same character, each team should also select an alternate for each round so that there can be a new face-off without going back into a new huddle.)

We play until one team totally engulfs the other (or until the Body Snatchers invade and devour everyone). ■

Swamp Chute

This game has nothing to do with shooting alligators in a swamp. That's illegal because alligators are an endangered species. Our game treats these critters very kindly by transforming a parachute into a great swampy home for them. And since these 'gators seem to have hearty appetites, the endangered species in this game turns out to be the humans.

We all hold on to the edge of a parachute and sit down with our legs under the chute. That's a very unwise move, it will turn out, because one of us has snuck under the chute to become a toothy alligator who hasn't had a square meal in days.

Worse yet, we can't really tell where the hungry beast is, because we're just having fun billowing the chute while chanting the name of our favorite

tropical swamp. (If we haven't got a favorite swamp, Okefenokee has a nice ring to it.)

The first warning we have of the alligator peril is likely to be one of our number letting out a bone-chilling yell as he's grabbed by the legs by *something* pulling him under into the swampy muck. We never see him again. Shortly thereafter, we get the feeling that there are now two alligators operating in our swamp, because two more of us soon disappear into the mire with barely a chance to cry out for help.

One could almost imagine that there are now *four* hungry 'gator denizens of our parachute swamp, the way our numbers are being devoured with geometric frequency. The natural progression of this game is obvious and inevitable. Now, what's a good game for fifty voracious alligators all slithering under a billowing, sunlit parachute swamp?

More Parachute Games. A parachute is perhaps our most playful single piece of equipment. All we have to do is haul one out and everyone seems to gravitate toward it, take hold, and start inventing games. There are a number of great parachute games described in *The New Games Book* and here are a few more.

We can play Cat and Mouse by billowing the chute from around the edges while one or more of us, as mice, crawl around underneath. Several cats scamper about on top of the chute and try to catch them. If we're proficient billowers, we can create quite a challenge for those cats.

Or we can do Paracalisthenics. We can perform a rotational group situp by sitting around the chute with our legs underneath it and holding on tight. Or we can lie on our backs underneath the chute with our heads toward the center and with the

edge of the parachute tucked under our butts. That keeps our legs supported in an upright position. Now we all move our legs in a circular motion. If someone has had the foresight to bring a Nerf ball in with him under the chute, this a unique setup for Handball in the Round.

If we have two small parachutes available, we can form teams and play Chute Volley, tossing an object back and forth. How about trying for height, distance, and consecutive-toss records?

We don't really need elaborate games to enjoy the parachute, however. We've rarely encountered a group who didn't love simply to work in unison to send a rippling wave around the edge of the chute, or billow it high above their heads into a giant mushroom canopy, filtering the sunlight as it bathes everyone in a gentle breeze. ∎

Vortex

We used to wind down our play sessions by drawing everyone together in a giant spiral, "wrapped around each other, closer than the stars in Andromeda Galaxy." Spirals is the name of the game as it appeared in *The New Games Book*. It is still one of the most fitting ways to end a playful get-together, but we've discovered a way to escape our galactic black hole and move on to other corners of the cosmos with Vortex.

We all hold hands in a large circle, facing the center. The leader drops hands with the person on her left and guides the chain of hand-holding players clockwise around the inside of the circle. The last person in the chain (the person who was on the leader's left) remains stationary until the human spiral winds itself tightly toward the center.

When the leader has taken enough turns around the inside of the circle so that the spiral seems about to strangle itself in its own coil, the leader switches directions at the center and begins to lead the chain *counterclockwise* back out of the spiral. As we all let ourselves be pulled along, the outward-spiraling people pass between the inward-spiraling lines. The key point is the vortex, where each person makes a sharp turn and reverses direction, from clockwise inward spiraling to counterclockwise outward spiraling.

The leader can take us back into the depths of the vortex again while we maintain our human chain, or she can lead us into myriad other formations. How about some chanting or singing while we're on our playful journey? ■

Psychic Shake

This game can't be approached with our usual frivolity. It has to do with ESP and cosmic forces and the like, and everyone knows that we're supposed to take such phenomena very seriously.

Once we're all in the proper meditative frame of mind (maybe a few deep breaths will help), we each settle on a number—one, two or three—that feels right for us at the moment. No guidelines here, and no conferring with our neighbors; we just reflect a minute and each of us decides which of the numbers moves him the most.

We now get to discover our numerical soul mates. Without breaking the mood, we mingle and start shaking hands with one another. If my number is one, I shake your hand just once; if it's two, I shake twice; and I shake your hand three times if it's three. If we have different numbers, there is an unmistakable moment of tension as one of us tries to stop the shake while the other continues. But if we have the same number, we stop at the same time and we *know* we're in the same group. Those of us with the same number stick together and continue our search for others of like persuasion.

We should be careful not to break the silence. This game is based on nonverbal communication—almost a secret code. Amazingly, often as not we will psychically divide ourselves into three exactly equal groups. But don't just take this on faith—try for yourselves. ∎

Get Down

This good-time ritual has probably been performed at every New Games event since it was first introduced to us at the New Games Camp in Malibu, California. It has worked in situations you absolutely would not believe. It's bound to work again, if we give it our spirited best.

We start in a large circle facing each other. One of us struts into the center and, while swinging her shoulders and hips and pointing her fingers in each of the four appropriate directions, launches into the following chant:

And up (chew-chi-chew, chew-chi-chew, chew-chi-chew),
And down (chew-chi-chew, chew-chi-chew, chew-chi-chew),
To the right (chew-chi-chew, chew-chi-chew, chew-chi-chew),
To the left (chew-chi-chew, chew-chi-chew, chew-chi-chew).

(The "chew-chi-chew" part is that familiar wire-brush-on-snare-drum sound.)

The chanter now strolls over to one of us in the circle and in her hippest, most zoot-suity style says:

Hey, there! You're a real cool cat!
You've got a lot of this, and you've got a lot of that!
So come on in and get down!

Who could resist such an invitation? Both the chanter and her invitee strut into the center and (with the rest of us joining in) repeat the whole "chew-chi-chew" routine, probably with a bit more spirit since there are now two cool cats. After the ups, downs, rights, and lefts, they go back to the edge of the circle and each of them invites another would-be hipster with "a lot of this and a lot of that" to join them.

These four do their "chew-chi-chews," and then invite four more real cool cats into the circle. Those eight become sixteen; those sixteen become thirty-two; and after only six more rounds, we'll have 4096 people pointing, swinging, and wire-brushing (and that's more than the Lap Game world's record)! In twenty-one rounds, we'll have all of Brooklyn getting down, and in thirty-two-and-a-third rounds, we'll have every human on the planet playing together.

So come on in and *get down!* ∎

After the Fourth Tournament

During a very special weekend in May of 1976, 6000 people came to a valley in the Golden Gate National Recreation Area, north of San Francisco, to play New Games. At the Fourth New Games Tournament, they played favorites like Orbit, Slaughter, People Pass, and Snake-in-the-Grass, and they ended the day with a record-breaking Lap Game. Everyone was exhausted and exhilarated. Especially those of us at the New Games Foundation. After months of planning and organizing, the tournament was a huge success. That spring we also shipped The New Games Book to the printers and completed our slide show, "Play Hard, Play Fair, Nobody Hurt." We wondered where to go from there.

Even before the tournament, the reputation of New Games and the foundation was growing. People had begun to hear about New Games, and their queries and concerns were arriving in our office. "How can I learn more about New Games?" "Come and lead games for my group." "When are you going to have the next tournament?" There were also suggestions that we train people to lead New Games.

New Games Foundation staff, fall 1977

The idea of training others intrigued us. It seemed to be the answer to our "What Next?" question. Rather than conducting tournaments and leading games ourselves, we could teach others how to do it. They would gain the skills and understanding to put on their own events, and word of New Games would spread faster and more effectively. There was also a practical consideration: Training others in New Games could provide much needed income to help make the foundation self-supporting.

The foundation's executive director, Burton Naiditch; New Games and play enthusiast John O'Connell; and games designer Bernie de Koven set themselves the task of developing a training program. It was a gradual process. As we tried out their ideas at various New Games events, we learned more about what people would need to know if they were going to spread the New Games message. It wouldn't be enough, for instance, just to know a few games and jump out and lead them, for New Games had things to say about the notion of leadership, the model of teamwork, and empowerment. Our experiments with the training program underlined the importance of game change, the wide applicability of New Games, and their power to create a feeling of community. And in order to give participants a chance to practice what they learned and to expose others to New Games, the idea of community festivals, to be held in conjunction with the trainings, was developed.

In the fall of 1976, we were ready to formally inaugurate the training program with our first open-training season. At four locations—in Pennsylvania, in New York, in Southern California and in Northern California—John, Burton, and Bernie's basic outline proved to be a workable model. All of about six people showed up at the first training, four of whom were friends of one of the trainers. A total of eighty came that season. Small though it was, a step had been taken that would determine and shape our energies for the next five years. We'd had small grants up to that point, but a three-year grant from the Charles Stewart Mott Foundation late in 1977 provided crucial seed money to fully develop the program and play the training game in a big way.

With each training season, we were able to improve the training program. As we refined it, we recruited more people to conduct the trainings. The nationwide training team numbered eleven at the first New Games Trainers Conference in 1978, held at the Marin Headlands in California. By the following summer, when the second trainers conference was held in Estes Park, Colorado, the training staff had grown to twenty. Reestablishing very special bonds and reaffirming a commitment to New Games, they refined the training program into its present form. New Games trainers are a very special and essential part of the New Games family. As different as they are in lifestyles and professions, they share a common belief in the magic of New Games—the spark that the freedom to play ignites in each of us. This is one of the basic motivations they share in conducting New Games trainings: to bring about a rediscovery in the joy of play. A listing of this unique group of player/trainers is found on page 189.

In the five years since the Fourth Tournament, New Games has become a strong recreation movement across the United States; it has reached Canada, Australia, the British Isles, and many European countries as well.

The training program began as a dream, romantic and practical at the same time. We started with a large-scale tournament that was played in one city and envisioned the same thing happening in a thousand cities. We started with an organization that had spent most of its energies delivering programs for little or no money and conceived for it a self-supporting activity. We started with a belief in the value of play and imagined people in communities everywhere changing their attitudes toward competition, trust, power, safety, leadership, risk, limitations, creativity, and participation. The training-program dream became a reality, and it continues to be our most effective way of communicating the idea of New Games.

New Games Trainers Conference, 1979, Estes Park, Colorado

New Games Training,
Cincinnati, Ohio

184 **A New Games Training.** *Since that first open training in fall 1976, more than 14,000 people have shared two or three days with us in almost 100 cities across the United States. If you decide to join us, you'll find that a New Games Training is unlike any other workshop you've ever attended.*

You'll begin by playing just for the sake of playing and having fun. You'll be surprised how easy it will be to lose yourself in the laughter and interactions as you move from one game to another. You'll play active and not-so-active games; you'll play indoors and outdoors, in small groups and large groups;

you'll change teams, change roles, change leaders, and even change games; you'll pretend and pantomime, take risks and try something new, trust and be trusted; you'll enjoy the freedom to quit or join a game, to be It or to not be It; you'll play hard and your play will help create a shared experience filled with camaraderie. Each play session at a training is different, but they're always fun.

Leading New Games is really nothing more than sharing your playfulness. At your training you'll have the chance to practice leading some of your fellow trainees in a game or two, and you'll learn some important techniques to help you. You'll learn to look at a game in terms of its components; you'll learn to be sensitive to the needs of your players; you'll learn about making changes in a game so that everyone can play together, even if your group includes children, chair-

bound players, and seniors. You'll also create games—through modifying an old game, combining two games, or inventing one from scratch.

There will be a celebration at your training that you will host. At the end of each training a festival is held for the surrounding community. You and your fellow trainees will join together to pass on the magic of New Games and gain experience in games leadership.

During the training you'll meet others in related professional areas or with similar personal interests. You'll share your ideas and resources for applying both the games and the concepts of New Games as you collectively solve the problems presented by different situations. The networking list you'll sign when you arrive at the training will be yours to take home. You'll have a whole list of supporters to call upon for help or a word of encouragement as you get ready for that school play day, or that staff in-service training, or that company picnic or neighborhood play session you're planning.

The people you'll get to know at the training will also become your friends. Throughout the training, you'll share a great deal: laughing together, playing with and against each other, doing something silly in one game and something risky in another, saying things you never thought you'd say in a group, sharing a potluck lunch, and practicing your new expertise in leading New Games at a festival of players. It will be a weekend of learning and playing, giving and taking, talking and listening, trusting and being trusted, supporting and being supported. You'll become a very special group of people, so don't be surprised to find that it's hard to say goodbye on Sunday afternoon.

The New Games Foundation conducts two- and three-day weekend trainings every spring in cities across the United States. They're open to everyone, and we'd love to have you join us. Let us know if you'd like our latest schedule.

185

New Games Training and Festival, Central Park, New York City
(in cooperation with New York City Department of Parks and Recreation)

186 **Group Trainings.** *In addition to our open trainings, we conduct group trainings on a contract basis. They are ideal for training the staff of a single organization. We've tailored our basic training format to meet the needs of over 100 groups, including Salem, Oregon, public schools; Eastman Kodak Company; Virginia Department of Corrections; Fairview, California, State Hospital; and Sudbury, Ontario, Parks and Recreation.*

We can adjust a group training to concentrate on your particular staff, your clientele, your environment. Perhaps you need a game-change session that focuses on adapting games for the physically disabled, or a refereeing session that centers on playing with juvenile deliquents, or an extended-application discussion that offers programing ideas for staff development, or festival preparation for a large citywide New Games Day. We approach our training program with an attitude of flexibility, and a group training gives us the opportunity to create a learning experience that's just what your organization needs.

Consulting Services. *We've found that New Games can be a tool that will assist human-services professionals in a variety of settings. Through our consulting service, we design special New Games programs to fit the needs of these professionals.*

For the disabled, New Games can be a therapeutic tool. We can provide access to play for the physically disabled, and opportunities for expressing more open behavior for the mentally disabled. In the inner city, New Games can be used as an organizing tool to foster community identity, open doors of communication, and build self-esteem among individuals. In the schools, New Games can improve intergroup relations and serve as a

vehicle to meet Title IX nondiscrimination requirements and special education needs. On the job, via employee programs, New Games can be helpful in stress management, fitness, and relaxation programs, and particularly in building teamwork and communication among employees. For seniors, New Games can provide resocialization, safe physical activity, and a time for interaction with peers, family, and community.

In all of these situations, we specifically modify games for our clients, conduct play sessions, and teach them the skills that will enable them to use New Games in long-term programing. We invite you to contact us if you'd like our help in applying New Games to your work/play setting.

Group training, Fairview State Hospital, Costa Mesa, California

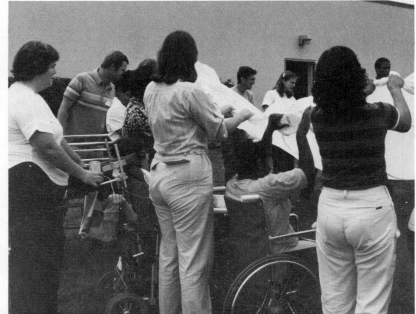

Play workshop, Doubleday &
Company, New York, New York

New Games Camps. *Over the years, we've been experimenting with a different kind of New Games experience. We know that when people come together to play, even for an hour, something special develops: a sense of community based on play. At our five-day residential camps we explore what happens when we don't have to stop playing to go home.*

Each of the eleven camps we've held so far has been unique, shaped by its participants. Week-long play offers a chance to live out fantasies, experience new challenges, and create shared folklore and ritual. Camp is a sleepless week of play and craziness, friendships and challenges, insights into playfulness and strong bonds to a very special play community.

Field Representatives. *The New Games Foundation has 48 certified representatives in the United States and Canada who are knowledgeable about New Games, skilled as leaders and willing to make a commitment to fostering New Games in their area. Our field representatives disseminate New Games to local communities. They conduct events and play sessions through our referrals and locally generated contacts; we offer them support by providing materials, discounts and some insurance coverage. This extension of the New Games Foundation family is one of the best vehicles we have for making New Games more accessible to more people.*

New Games Summer Camp, 1980,
Estes Park, Colorado

Funding the Foundation. *The New Games Foundation, a non-profit organization founded in 1974, is supported primarily by fees from the training program along with sales revenues and donations. The training program is the core of our activities. Just as grant monies enabled us to develop and refine that program, we continue to look for outside support to reach new audiences.*

The foundation's mail-order sales program currently offers The New Games Book, More New Games!, *Earthballs, playchutes, and a selection of T-shirts. We also rent our slide show, "Play Hard, Play Fair, Nobody Hurt."* The New Games Resource Catalog *is an annotated compilation of play ideas, books, equipment, and other resources.*

The items listed are all available directly through the manufacturer or publisher.

We have many dreams of ways we would like to further New Games. We're in need of grants or contributions to subsidize group trainings for special populations and support model programs for the consulting services described above. We'd also like to develop more audio-visual products and conduct research projects. As an organization whose purpose is to promote play through New Games, our potential activities are as endless as a list of New Games. Financial assistance is crucial if we are to make our dreams realities.

Friends of New Games. *Friends of New Games is our membership program. In becoming a member, you affirm a belief in play and join a community of players who share that belief. As a member you can take advantage of discounts on our services and products. Your tax-deductible membership donations provide much needed financial support and let us explore new program directions and reach more people.*

We believe play is an important part of life and that it begins within each of us. We invite you to join us in the New Games community. Together we can rediscover our own playfulness, share it with others, and create a game with limitless players, endless boundaries, and infinite joys.

—Nancy Kretz, Executive Director, New Games Foundation

NEW GAMES FOUNDATION

The purpose of the New Games Foundation is to foster and communicate a style of play that focuses on participation, creativity, and community. Through our trainings, play sessions, events, sales, and special programs, we've reached thousands of people. None of this would have been possible without the dedication of many hard-working and play-loving friends. Here is a list of the principal players in the foundation's Big Game for the past five years.

FAMILY OF PLAYERS, 1976-1981

Executive Director

Nancy Kretz

Former

Pam Cleland, 1980–1981
John O'Connell, 1977–1979
Burton Naiditch, 1976–1979

Staff

Bob Leavitt

Dave Koreski

Former

Peter Armour
Adrienne Burk
Bill Burke
Joyce Carr
Bernie de Koven
Richard Halstead
Paul Herron
Larry Loebig

Kitty McKenna
Trina Merriman
Barbara Naiditch
Kathryn Parker
Sheila Stone
Todd Strong
Debrah Woodbey

Board of Directors

David Bland
Jim Dutcher
Andy Grimstad

Ray Murray
Marcia Taylor
Marcelle Weed

Former

David Aikman
Nellie Arnold
Peter Ellis
Andrew Fluegelman

Jadine Nielson
Julia Robb
Michael Toms

Trainers

Betsy Brown
Steve Butler
Pam Cleland
Jean Harrison
Bill Healey
Joe Killian
Nancy Kretz
Ken Leary
Jeff McKay
Trina Merriman
Bill Michaelis

Juliette Moore
Carolyn Muegge
Burton Naiditch
John O'Connell
Lainey Reiss
Gail Straub
Todd Strong
Marcelle Weed
John Wertz
Tom Zink

Former

Dave Bacon
Chuck Conn
Soozy Conrad
Bernie de Koven
Kate Douglas

Dale LeFevre
Jan Lown
David Naster
Bruce Werber

Field Representatives

Laura Alfano
Jane Ander
Dave Bacon
Ron Ball
Mike Berman
Arnie Biondo
Betsy Brown
Adrienne Burk
Steve Butler
Vic Chaisson
Kate Douglas
Fred Evers
Allen Feld
Jim Given
Corinne Graham
Jean Harrison
Bill Healey
Bev Hoffman
Linda Jimenez
Joe Killian
Ken Leary
Larry Loebig
Jan Lown
Jeff McKay

Mary Lou Massey
Trina Merriman
Bill Michaelis
Juliette Moore
Kathryn Parker
Lainey Reiss
John Rippey
Ruthanne Robinette
Bill Rubin
Joan Rupert
Lee Rush
Martin Schwartz
Charlie Steffens
Gail Straub
Todd Strong
Shay Tindall
C.L. Tree
Neal Watzman
Marcelle Weed
John Wertz
Karen Wolf
Gayle Wulk
Bill Yoskowitz
Tom Zink

NEW GAMES...
AND MORE!

Page numbers in *italic* type refer to *The New Games Book*.
Page numbers in roman type refer to *More New Games!*

	High Activity	Medium Activity	Low Activity
Games for Two	Boffing 25	Butt Off 23	Aura *37*
	Crab Grab 15	Fraha *33*	Commons 25
	Human Spring 17	Hunker Hawser *31*	Frisbee Golf *39*
	Schmerltz *27*	Me Switch 19	Last Detail 29
	Toe Fencing 13	New Frisbee *29*	Stand-Off *35*
	Tweezli-Whop *23*	Quick Draw 21	This Is My Nose 27
Games for a Dozen	Bola 49	Ball Crawl 67	A What? 73
	Catch the Dragon's Tail *47*	Behavior Modification 63	The Bone Game *79*
	Flying Dutchman *45*	Fox and Squirrel 59	Egg Toss 75
	Frisbee Fakeout 47	Group Juggling 61	Instant Replay 71
	Go-Tag *53*	How Do You Do? 57	Killer 81
	Human Pinball *51*	People Pyramids *57*	Knots *69*
	Samurai Warrior 51	Pieing 63	Lummi Sticks *73*
	Star Wars 55	Pile Up 65	Mime Rhyme 83
	Swat 45	Pushpin Soccer 69	Name Train 75
	Taffy Pull 49	Smaug's Jewels *61*	Rattlers 77
	Triangle Tag 43	Snowblind 59	Red Handed *71*
	Ultimate Nerf 53	Stand Up 65	Sightless Sculpture 77
	Water Slide 55	Willow in the Wind 67	Zen Clap *79*
Games for Two Dozen	Blob *107*	Body Snatchers 125	Data Processing 139
	British Bulldog *105*	Body Surfing 133	Elephant/Palm Tree/Monkey 147
	Broken Spoke 105	Bug Tug *121*	Hagoo *135*
	Clam Free 113	Caterpillar *117*	Human Compressor 141
	Dho-Dho-Dho *97*	Cookie Machine 135	Islands *127*
	Elbow Tag 121	Hug Tag *115*	Knight's Move 137
	Great Plains *99*	Jamaquack 129	The Mating Game *125*
	Knock Your Socks Off 117	Lemonade 127	Ooh-Ahh *129*
	Loose Caboose 107	New Volleyball *113*	Pina *131*
	Monarch 115	Orbit *111*	Prui *133*
	Siamese Soccer *95*	Quick Lineup 131	Rain 149
	Snake-in-the-Grass *93*	Rock/Paper/Scissors *109*	Shoe Factory 143
	Slaughter/Annihilation *101*	Skin the Snake *119*	Tableaux 145
	Wink 109	Yurt Circle 123	Vampire *123*
The More the Better	Clench a Wench/Mensch *151*	Amoeba Race *159*	Eco-Ball *175*
	Earth Volley *155*	Chute Ball *165*	Get Down 179
	Earthball Games *143*, 162	Giants/Elves/Wizards 167	The Lap Game *171*
	Everybody's It 159	Parachute Games *161*, 173	Planet Pass *167*
	Octopus 157	People Pass *157*	Psychic Shake 177
	Space Chase 161	People to People 165	Spirals 169
	Tug of War *153*	Swamp Chute 171	Vortex 175

Copyright © 1981 by The Headlands Press, Inc.

What's Your New Game?

Do you have a favorite game you'd like to share?
Please let us know about it.
Or tell us about a variation of one of the games in this book.
We'll pass it along to the New Games community.

Name of game: _____

How it's played:

☐ My organization is interested in
   sponsoring a group training.
☐ Enclosed is $1.00 for the *New Games
   Resource Catalog* that gives ordering
   information for:
   ☐ *More New Games!*
   ☐ Earthballs
   ☐ Playchutes
   ☐ T-shirts
   ☐ Slide-show rental
   ☐ Other books and play equipment

Name _____

Address _____

City _____

State _____ Zip _____

Phone _____

Organization_____

My primary field of interest is:
☐ Recreation   ☐ Business
☐ Education   ☐ Health
☐ Youth   ☐ Church
☐ Other_____

Mail this form to:
New Games Foundation
P.O. Box 7901
San Francisco, California 94120

cut

_____

_____

_____

**New
Games
Foundation**

P.O. Box 7901
San Francisco, California 94120